THE APPLICATION OF MODERN SYSTEMATIC MANAGEMENT

This is a volume in the
Arno Press collection

HISTORY OF MANAGEMENT THOUGHT

See last pages of this volume
for a complete list of titles

THE APPLICATION OF MODERN SYSTEMATIC MANAGEMENT

Edited by
Alfred D. Chandler

ARNO PRESS
A New York Times Company
New York • 1979

Editorial Supervision: BRIAN QUINN
Reprint Edition 1979 by Arno Press Inc.

HISTORY OF MANAGEMENT THOUGHT
AND PRACTICE
ISBN for complete set: 0-405-12306-X
See last pages of this volume for titles.

Manufactured in the United States of America

Library of Congress Cataloging in Publication Data
Main entry under title:

The Application of modern systematic management.

(History of management thought)
Articles reprinted from System.
1. Industrial management--United States--Addresses, essays, lectures. I. Chandler, Alfred Dupont. II. Series.
HD70.U5A76 658'.00973 79-7522
ISBN 0-405-12307-8

CONTENTS

Leffingwell, W[illiam] H.
MY PLAN FOR APPLYING "SCIENTIFIC MANAGEMENT" IN AN OFFICE (Reprinted from *System: The Magazine of Business,* vol. 30, no. 4) October, 1916

Leffingwell, W[illiam] H.
THIS PLAN MORE THAN DOUBLED OUR TYPISTS' OUTPUT (Reprinted from *System: The Magazine of Business,* vol. 30, no. 5) November, 1916

Leffingwell, W[illiam] H.
WHAT "SCIENTIFIC MANAGEMENT" DID FOR MY OFFICE (Reprinted from *System: The Magazine of Business,* vol. 30, no. 6; vol. 31, no. 1) December, 1916, January, 1917

Leffingwell, W[illiam] H.
41 WAYS TO SAVE TIME IN AN OFFICE
(Reprinted from *System: The Magazine of Business,* vol. 31, no. 2) February, 1917

HOW I MADE A SUCCESS OF MY BUSINESS

Henry Ford

HE INCREASED HIS BUSINESS 26,400% IN 11 YEARS

Henry Ford has built up within a comparatively short period a business that now shows net profits of about $1,000,000 a week. An interesting article by him – "How I Made a Success of My Business" – begins on the opposite page

SYSTEM
THE MAGAZINE OF BUSINESS

VOLUME XXX NOVEMBER, 1916 NUMBER 5

How I Made a Success of My Business

By HENRY FORD

ELEVEN years ago the company Henry Ford heads and controls was making less than 2,000 cars a year; now it produces well over 530,000 annually – a 26,400% increase in about a decade. Ford was close to forty when work began on the eighth Ford car; he has not turned fifty-four yet, and his company's assets are nearing the $100,000,000 mark.

Thus there can be no denial of Henry Ford's success – perhaps his, indeed, is America's most outstanding individual business success – and so his business methods are naturally of interest. But since he apparently gives particular importance to certain fundamental principles, the question at once arises: "Can these principles be adapted to the every-day conditions encountered in large and small businesses?"

Perhaps the best way to answer this question is to mention two incidents from a type of business quite unlike manufacturing automobiles. The statement that follows, for instance, was made by a merchant – Theodore G. Morgan, of Henry Morgan and Company, a Canadian concern which operates a large department store: "One of the great secrets of the Ford organization has been specialization. . . . . There is a great lesson in retailing to be gained from this point." The second incident has to do with a Boston store. Ford declares that any man, regardless of what line he is in, can make a fortune if he can produce something the people want in quantities and hold down expenses. One of the most successful stores in New England has taken over this idea and specializes on lines that are familiarly known among its buyers as "Ford BB's" ("Ford Best in Boston").

Believing that these and a number of similar incidents indicate the practical usefulness of additional information on Ford methods, SYSTEM asked Mr. Ford for an article. He consented, and it was arranged for Martyn Johnson to transcribe the interview. The Ford Motor Company also generously agreed to make a member of SYSTEM's staff "guest free" for several weeks, and from this arrangement there developed an interesting series which will start in SYSTEM for December

THERE is one principle which a man must follow if he wishes to succeed, and that is to understand human nature. I am convinced by my own experience, and by that of others, that if there is any secret of success it lies in the ability to get another person's point of view and see things from his angle as well as from your own.

It makes no difference if a man employs ten men or ten thousand, the success of his business will be in direct proportion to his understanding of human nature. I would even go so far as to say that this faculty is the business man's greatest asset.

It is easy enough to say: "Understand human nature," but it takes a lot of hard thinking and constant thinking really to get at the significance of that remark.

WHY IT PAYS AN EMPLOYER TO "TAKE THOUGHT" OF HIS EMPLOYEES

What do I mean by saying that success depends upon the ability to understand people? Well, in the first place, an employer must understand the people working for him. He must not make the mistake of thinking of them as units or wage earners or as being in any way different from himself. If he is going to get their best work and effort, their interest, and consequently the best results in his business, he has got to realize that he has human beings working for him who have the same ambitions and desires that he has.

Every one of us, no matter who or what we are, wants to succeed. Now when an employer begins to see his employees in this light he has gone a long way toward success in business, for what happens? He begins instinctively to understand that the success of his workmen and the success of his business are tied up together and he will begin to wonder how his men can best succeed in his business.

He will discover that one man can do one thing better than another, or one group of men, and they will be shifted to that particular kind of work. And just notice what is happening in that business organization: the employer is specializing, he is getting the right people in the right place where they can work to the best advantage not only to themselves but to the whole business. Don't ever forget that the welfare of any business and the welfare of the individual workers are just as closely related to one another as the law of cause and effect. This is the law of cause and effect of business success.

And, after all, this is simply common sense. There is no denying that a man who works with enthusiasm and interest is going to earn a lot more for his employer than the man who is indifferent and discouraged, if only the employer will give him a chance.

I wish I could say to every employer in the country: Remember that your workmen are human beings with ambition to succeed exactly like yourself. Give them a chance in your business to serve their own self-interest in serving yours. Make them valuable to you by giving them a chance to become valuable to themselves. There is no way under the sun to get valuable employees except by giving them a chance to get ahead for themselves.

Now you can't fool anyone along this line. A man may have a lot of fine talk about having the interests of his workmen at heart, but if it is not there in fact and deed, his men will know it and he will not get their support.

It is the easiest thing in the world to inspire this loyalty, but it's not to be done by any trick. It's simply a matter of honest and sincere understanding of the workman's interests, a recognition of his ambitions as a human being. If your men feel that is your attitude toward them, they will do their best work every hour of the day.

WHAT DOES "SERVING THE PUBLIC" REALLY MEAN?

The trouble with a great many of us in the business world is that we are thinking hardest of all about the dollars we want to make. Now that is the wrong idea right at the start.

If people would go into business with the idea that they are going to serve the public and their employees as well as themselves, they would be assured of success from the very start. Everything connected with such a business enterprise

ONE OF THE FORD "SCHOOLS"

"A man who works with enthusiasm and interest is going to earn a lot more for his employer than the man who is indifferent and discouraged, if only the employer will give him a chance"

would work toward its success and the money would come in without any worry on the part of anyone.

Now this suggests another idea along the same line. The business man who wants to succeed must, on the one hand, understand his employees and so organize his business that each man in doing the best he can for his employer is also doing the best he can for himself; and, on the other hand, he must apply exactly the same principle to the public.

He must make the public serve him in serving itself. By that I mean he must render the public a genuine service in selling it his products. The public is quick to get a sense of confidence, but it is just as quick to lose it when there is cause. Just let a man take advantage of the public for his own selfish interest and see!

The great chance for success lies in finding out what the public needs, and right here comes in the ability to understand human nature. The next step after finding out something that is necessary to people's welfare is to make that article the very best you can and sell it as cheap as you can, no matter if it be shoes or automobiles. Make something that the people need and make it so good that they want to buy your particular product; actually render them a service by selling them that article.

I tell you the man who has this idea of service in his business will never need to worry about profits. The money is bound to come. This idea of service in business is the biggest guarantee of success that any man can have.

One of the first things that a man has to learn in business is how little he can do by himself. When he finds that out he begins to look around for people to do what he can't. He begins to study people, he begins to see that everyone has something good in him and he begins to cooperate with the good qualities in the people about him.

I believe in this idea of cooperation in business and I believe in big business organization. The bigger the business the bigger the chance to harness up a lot of people with special ability. And in this idea of specialization lies the chance of perfection, and perfection means success.

The more you think about anything, the more you understand it; you get special information about it, and the more special information you have the better you are equipped to meet competition. It's the man who is the ablest specialist in his line who wins the biggest success.

Everyone of us can do some one thing very well, but none can do a lot of things well at the same time. Perhaps he will do them as well as other people, but that idea of doing things as well as other people has no place in business. We have got to do things better than other people if we are going to win out.

I am sure that it would pay a firm to do one single thing, say make one particular size in boots. If one factory devoted its entire energy to making one size in boots, millions and millions of pairs exactly alike, think of the saving in time and energy! And what was saved in time and energy could be put into the perfecting of that particular boot, so that

WHAT WILL THE NEXT FORD SURPRISE BE?

"Make something that the people need and make it so good that they want to buy your particular product; actually render them a service by selling them that article"

WHAT FORD BELIEVES MAKES SUCCESS SURE

"If people would go into business with the idea that they are going to serve the public and their employees as well as themselves, they would be assured of success from the very start"

it could be made the best and the cheapest boot in the world.

I can't say too often that it is thinking that counts in business. A man who wants to get ahead must be thinking about everything that comes his way: about the people he employs, the people he works with, the people to whom he sells.

Everything in this world is tied up in one way or another with everything else, and a man can get a million side lights on his own specialty if he is always awake to its relationship with the rest of the world. Everything in the successful business is evolved by thinking, everything starts with a thought; and this habit of analysis, this ability to get under the surface of things, to get at the vital essentials, gives a man a tremendous advantage over those of his competitors who do not do likewise.

There is not one single detail in business today but can be improved by thinking. We have not reached perfection in any line. Improvement means increased success, and improvement is the result of thinking. The great trouble in business today is that most people are so busy doing a variety of things that they have not time to get a real grip on any one thing.

Now weeds are a very good illustration of what I have been saying about business. For centuries people have thought that weeds were perfectly useless. Farmers have spent time and money pulling them up, burning them up, anything to get rid of them.

DO BUSINESS MEN THINK AND READ AS MUCH AS THEY SHOULD?

But now comes along a man who has been thinking about weeds, analyzing and experimenting, and what does he find out? That weeds are the best fertilizer for the soil and that instead of spending money to enrich his fields, all the farmer has to do is to plow the weeds under!

Think of all the money that has been spent, the time wasted, in destroying weeds which contain the very chemicals the farmer has been buying in the form of fertilizers! And all because the farmer took it for granted that weeds were his enemy and never stopped to do some special thinking!

Now this principle of specialization applies to the small employer just as well as to the large. If a small manufacturer begins to do some special thinking he will get big ideas about his work and as he follows those up in practice his business will grow accordingly.

I started that way. I had an idea and I thought about it. I kept on thinking, and I'm still thinking.

Why, the first man I ever hired was a fellow I knew. He's still with me. Why did I hire that particular man? Because I knew him, I knew what he could do. I saw that he had something I needed. Cooperation, you see, but on a small scale.

The boy we hired to run errands and sweep out the shop is now our head chemist. I didn't hire him with any idea that he could ever be a chemist. He didn't know anything about chemistry when I hired him. But I got to know him while he was working around the shop. As business grew he had more to do. He naturally grew as he had more to do.

I found out there were certain things he could do better than others and I put him on those jobs. Then the time came when we needed someone to make steel tests. We found that the steel we were getting was not always up to the samples.

So he was sent down to the mills to learn all about steel and how to analyze it and make the tests. He began to do some of this special thinking I have been talking about.

He still is. He has found out a lot of things we never knew about steel. Special thinking, that's what it has been from the start with us. Anyone else can do the same thing if he works the same way.

My advice to every business man is to read a lot and think a lot and work a lot. If he will think and think and keep on thinking, and follow up his thinking with work, he is certain to succeed.

But he must not fail to think about people as well as things. He must understand human nature, as I said at the start. And the best way to understand human nature is to be friendly toward people. Everyone has some good in him and the man that has that attitude toward people will find their good qualities, and it's those qualities he wants to use in his business.

WHY CRITICISM IS VALUABLE TO THE BUSINESS MAN

And one thing more. No business man ought ever to be afraid of criticism. Just as sure as he tries to do anything different, he will stir up a lot of criticism.

But criticism is exactly like those weeds I was talking about – full of valuable fertilization. Just plow it under and let it fertilize your thinking. Criticism is the best educator in the world. Everything I have learned has been through criticism and the thinking it induced in me.

WHAT'S BEHIND FORD'S $1,000,000 A WEEK?

Harry Franklin Porter

HOW WORK KEEPS COMING

One of the policies in the Ford factories is to time each job so it moves ahead to the next workman just when he is ready for it. Thus the work, as here in the piston department, goes through at a predetermined speed

WHAT'S BEHIND FORD'S $1,000,000 A WEEK?

Last month Henry Ford himself described in SYSTEM some of the policies responsible for his success – this article is the first of a series that will tell in greater detail about the methods used in his plant

BY HARRY FRANKLIN PORTER — *Illustrated with* PHOTOGRAPHS

WITHIN a comparatively short time Henry Ford has built up a concern that annually nets over $52,000,000. For this reason, if for no other, his business methods are of interest.

We know that he has followed very definite policies, for by nature he is evidently a man who takes a definite stand. Since these policies have proved so tremendously successful for Ford, the question of whether or not they can be adapted to other activities than automobile making, and to small concerns as well as large, is of importance.

Ford has said that his methods can be used in practically all lines. There are, furthermore, instances on record of their adaptation to the requirements of businesses quite unlike an automobile business. For example, one successful retail establishment is merchandising some of its lines according to Ford fundamentals and makes special stocks of dresses under Ford principles. A furniture factory is manufacturing chairs according to a typical Ford practice. Theodore G. Morgan of Henry Morgan and Company – a long-established Canadian retail house – says: "One of the great secrets of the Ford organization has been specialization. . . . . . There is a great lesson in retailing to be gained from this point."

On page 599 a series of articles begins which will analyze and describe Ford's methods. The Ford Motor Company very generously made SYSTEM's representative in charge of the series –

Harry Franklin Porter – "guest free" at its plant in Detroit for several weeks. Every effort has been taken to assure the accuracy of the articles, Mr. Ford himself having gone over the following article. In introducing the series with an article by him published in SYSTEM for November, Mr. Ford said: "I had an idea and I thought about it. I kept on thinking, and I'm still thinking."

COMMENTING upon the over-emphasis that has been placed by various workers in the field of management upon some one or other branch of the subject, Boyd Fisher, vice-president of the Executives' Club of Detroit, has this to say in regard to the Ford Motor Company: "It is thinkable that two whole new theories of management, touching none of the points of the Taylor system of scientific management, should come out of the Ford plant alone. A treatise, for instance, might be written on the subdivision of labor and progressive machining and assembling, because these elements of management as developed at the Ford plant have had as much to do with increasing output and lowering the cost of production as the Taylor system has had in other plants.

"Perhaps they have decreased costs more than the Taylor system has. The other phase of management in which the Ford plant has had an equal influence is the theory of social regulation, the method of creating a new temper in the working force and making the whole body of workers more efficient, not so much as workers, but as *Men*. Nevertheless, a treatise on management written from the point of view of the Ford plant alone would be vastly incomplete for other plants, because there are whole areas of scientific management knowledge and method for which Ford obviously has little need."

Mr. Fisher has undoubtedly placed his finger upon the two most remarkable features of the Ford organization – how practical continuity is achieved in a naturally discontinuous industry, and how the workers individually and as a body are controlled from the standpoint of social as well as of industrial effectiveness. These two features have a wide interest and are worthy the close study of all manufacturers.

But there are many other elements that, while perhaps less spectacular, may also be studied with considerable profit. In fact, on almost whatever branch of the great Ford organization the microscope of observation and analysis is turned, methods of dealing with problems common to all business are often found which are alike interesting, unique and adaptable in a greater or less degree to other plants.

WHERE THE STRENGTH OF THE FORD ORGANIZATION LIES

Nor are these features of general interest and profit confined to the manufacturing side alone. Sales and advertising, traffic, purchasing, financing, accounting and administrative methods in general all present a number of features which are fully as different, as noteworthy and as advanced. In fact, the Ford Motor Company presents an unusually good example of a well-balanced organization throughout. Some concerns are strong on the engineering side, others on the manufacturing, still others on the sales side; elsewhere they are only fair, and often in one or two aspects decidedly inferior. Where they are weak they must become strong; where they are strong they must at least not lose strength, if cumulative success is to be achieved.

The best evidence of the degree of all-around development of the Ford organization is that by those with the selling slant on business it is regarded as a selling success, by production experts as a triumph for large scale production, specialization, standardization and subdivision of labor; while to those mechanically inclined the shop equipment and practice looms up large. Inventors ascribe most to Ford's own work as a designing engineer. Financiers speak of his work as a financial achievement. And so it goes.

Is the Ford business chiefly a selling success? Yes and no. If steadily increasing sales, ever-widening distribution, constantly lessening selling costs, and an over-selling of the factory's capacity year after year, are evidences of a remarkably efficient sales organization – yes. On the other hand, if by selling success is meant the marketing of a product in spite of its shortcomings – no.

SOME OF FORD'S SELLING POLICIES, AND WHY THEY ARE EFFECTIVE

Perhaps the cardinal feature of the Ford selling scheme is the emphasis placed on service. Incessantly the fact is impressed upon the Ford branches and agencies, in the weekly sales bulletins, in the sales literature, in the sales letters, and by word of mouth from the selling chiefs, that they are not selling cars alone, but cars plus service. In the Ford factory, repair parts receive first consideration. It is related that at one time car production was totally discontinued for several days in order to catch up on the repair parts orders.

This is not to say that the Ford organization is one hundred per cent perfect in every respect. Perhaps it is not perfect in even any single point and the Ford managers would be the first to criticise any observer who called it perfect.

If one attitude stands in the way of effectiveness in the average plant, it is complacency, pride in the home establishment which blinds the producer to his own shortcomings, causes him to ignore the good points of others and to resent well-meant criticism. Not so in the Ford plant. From Ford on down, with insignificant exceptions, the men in authority are open minded, glad to receive suggestions, willing to profit by the wisdom and experience of others.

The attitude of Ford himself is well illustrated by an incident which happened at the Wayne Country Fair a year ago. The Ford Motor Company was among the exhibitors. One of the features of their exhibit was a practical demonstration of the new Ford tractor, which Ford hopes to place on the market soon.

The demonstration field was constantly crowded with curious sight-seers. A large proportion of them were farmers attracted principally by the opportunity to see the tractor at work. Ford made it his business to be on the ground to hear the comments.

One man came up to him and began to praise the Ford tractor. Ford stopped him. "Praise is not what I came out to hear," he said, in effect. "What I want you to tell me is where that machine is inefficient, where it falls down. In my own heart I am not yet satisfied that it is entirely right. I want you practical fellows to help me make it right. Tell me where it is wrong, not where it is all right. I don't care a rap about that."

While this attitude of the student, the learner, continues to dominate the Ford organization, the steady growth and development of the Ford factories may be taken for granted. Perhaps nothing is truer than that business institutions, as do individuals, usually progress only so long as they are open minded, willing and able to draw from the experiences of others, courageous to blaze the trail where precedent offers no guidance.

HOW NEW PLANS HAVE BEEN WORKED OUT

With Ford, indeed, it has been mostly a case of blazing new trails. In tackling some of the big problems which it has solved, the Ford organization has had little previous experience to serve as a guide. Yet that very fact has been an advantage to Ford. Workers in well-established fields are often altogether too prone to accept things as they find them and incorporate bodily into their practice methods and principles which, if given the acid test, would be found wanting.

"Henry Ford is so farsighted he sags in the middle," his friend Thomas Edison is reputed to have said. This quality

A SPECIAL MACHINE TO SUIT THE JOB

When the market does not provide machines which will do the work of the Ford factories as economically as the Ford engineers believe it can be done, it is not uncommon for them to design and build special equipment. Here, for example, is a specially-designed machine for making springs

Ford seems to have communicated to his entire organization. From managers and superintendents down to foremen, everyone appears to be looking ahead, to be on his mettle to discover and inaugurate changes which will increase output and reduce costs, and yet not jeopardize quality or service.

Unlike many pioneers, however, the Ford Motor Company has not sowed for others to come along and do all the reaping. Problems have been worked out for the benefit of the entire business world, but the Ford plant has of course attempted to extract every possible benefit itself. It has by no means rested on its oars while others profited from its experiences.

Canny business sense has tempered an unusually high percentage of the steps taken at the Ford plants. The golden mean of common sense, in fact, is its great single, outstanding and underlying characteristic. If one is looking to Ford for finely-spun systems, he will be disappointed; if, on the other hand, he has his eyes open for common-sense solutions of manufacturing, business and human problems, he will find much to delight him.

Change also permeates the Ford plant. New policies, new methods are continually being inaugurated. The superintendents think nothing of dismantling a whole department and moving it bodily. The visitor of today who goes through

WHERE SPENDING IS ECONOMY

At the Ford plant they interpret "economy" broadly. Not long ago this room contained a perfect forest of belts, but now each machine has been equipped – at great expense – with individual motor drive, because it seemed wise to have each unit independent

the plant tomorrow or next week might hunt in vain for a department the location and character of which he had definitely fixed in his mind.

For instance, the pressed steel department, once the largest single department in the plant, has been disintegrated. This was once prescribed by Ford's policy, inaugurated some time ago, of having each part manufactured complete in a department. So, in the future, the pressed steel work, instead of being concentrated in one area, will be scattered throughout the shop, the presses being interspersed in logical order with other machines performing preceding or succeeding operations on a part.

Another noteworthy Ford change is concerned with the individual motor drive. At one time the Ford machine shop was a perfect forest of belts. Here and there you will find large open spaces now. A closer inspection will reveal the fact that overhead shafting and belt drive have given way to local motor drive, with the belts – if there are any – extending only from the shaft of a motor, mounted on some part of the frame of a machine, to the driving pulley of the machine below.

All new machines are thus equipped. Now that Ford's forty-five-thousand-horse-power plant is completed, all his old machines will be changed over. In certain cases, groups of similar machines will continue to be shaft-and-belt driven, from a large, centrally-positioned motor, but in general Ford's intention is to make each machine independent, even though economy of operation might lie on the side of group drive.

Back of this change is the same broad-gauged interpretation of economy that characterizes the conduct of the entire Ford plant. While some others are debating the relative merits of individual as

WHERE FORD PLANS ARE SET GOING

Once it is decided that a change of some kind is desirable, there is no unnecessary delay in putting it through. These men who direct the work from the superintendent's office find the best way and promptly put it into effect

against group motor-drive, and splitting pennies to decide the question which never will be decided finally if it continues to be weighed on a narrow basis, the Ford engineers, looking beyond mere power economies and seeing the advantages of self-contained machine units, have settled definitely on the individual drive as wisest in their plant.

Freedom from overhead shafting and belting, with their obstructions of light, heavy friction losses and excessive maintenance expenses, and the attainment of an ability to shift machines around at will until a more effective arrangement of contiguous operations is achieved – these are the main reasons, in their opinion, justifying the change. Ford has not made this change before, largely because he had been too busy getting out production and making more important changes – the development of progressive machining and assembling, for instance.

One change usually leads to another, however, and as Ford's effort has been increasingly centered on the attainment of straight-line production and minimum space and time intervals between successive operations, the advantage of location afforded by individually motor-driven machines has become increasingly apparent to him.

"We find you never can achieve a thoroughly satisfactory layout with shafting and belting," declared one of his superintendents. "That is the reason why we are installing motors on all machines, except in isolated instances where group drive does not interfere with securing the best arrangement."

Incessant change, to some business men, is an evidence of an infirmity of purpose. Any change from the existing order is abhorrent to these men. "Let well enough alone," "it costs too much," "let's wait until next year," or "we can't afford it just now" – these are some of the arguments they advance.

From this kind of reasoning the Ford plant is singularly free. The spirit of progress is uppermost.

Once the benefit of a suggested improvement is seen and weighed, hesitation instantly vanishes, a decision is made promptly, action begins at once. The immediate cost usually cuts no figure with Ford, so long as the permanent good is undoubted.

WHY IT IS EASY TO GET PROMPT ACTION ON LARGE PROBLEMS

By this it might be taken that there is a good deal of precipitous action at the Ford plant. On the contrary, almost every move is carefully calculated. Decisions are prompt because responsibility is acutely centered in a small group of able men, all of whom are active in the business. There is no conservative board of directors to win over, no dominating financial interest to dictate. And once a decision is made, the execution of it is swift, because a well-trained and disciplined organization, backed by ample resources, is at the call of the heads.

Where leisurely procedure serves a good purpose, however, it is cheerfully tolerated. For instance, before undertaking to manufacture parts which previously have been made outside, the practical details of the processing are carefully worked out. Months of experimentation may intervene. Not until the superintendents are satisfied that they have perfected the method, and can produce at a saving, is regular manufacture attempted.

About a year ago, for instance, Ford began to manufacture his own springs on a small scale. A new machine has been developed which forms the leaves while they are tempering. It is confidently expected that this machine will show large savings. But the springs were not allowed to be used on the regular product at once. They were just put on cars owned by the company and by officials in order that they might first be thoroughly tried out.

Whether it is in starting to assemble motor cars on the fly or to link steam with gas engines in units of unprecedented size; or in pinning his faith to light car construction and to one model; or in setting out to produce gray and malleable iron directly from the blast furnace heat – when the iron experts said it couldn't be done; or in setting unusual quotas for the sales force; or in embarking in the motion picture business on a wholesale scale as a new method of advertising his product; or in studying human nature, making good citizens and good workmen out of foreigners, human derelicts and even criminals – no matter upon what part of the Ford organization your eye rests, you will usually find the unmistakable impress of this rare quality.

Henry Ford started out to make a product for the average man. At that time – and still, to a large extent – the output in his line was regarded as a luxury. Ford took a sharp issue with that point of view and has succeeded. That he sized up his market correctly needs no other proof than the statistics that trace the growth of his factories – a growth probably without parallel. The basis of this success is a rare ability to interpret the needs of the masses.

THERE ARE GOOD REASONS FOR SUCH GROWTH AS THIS

The growth of Ford's business is all the more remarkable when it is remembered that twenty-eight thousand dollars was the entire amount of his paid-in capital. No more has since been added from outside sources – every step has been financed out of earnings from an ever-increasing output with a continual lowering of sales prices. Ford's company has today assets which exceed one hundred millions of dollars.

Henry Ford and the small group of men who pooled their resources with his at the beginning have become multi-millionaires. Over a million and a half customers have dealt with Ford. A small army of employees – over forty thousand of them in the parent plant alone – get unusual wages from Ford.

There are additional startling facts about Ford's success that I might mention. Whatever stand one may personally take in regard to Ford's ideas and Ford's viewpoint, the fact remains that Ford has succeeded. Therefore, there is a natural desire to know about the methods by which he succeeded, what he is planning for the future, to whom he is going to leave his vast business, and so forth, and so on.

You will find in many instances that studying Ford himself is a good way to study the Ford business. He's quick on meeting the issue, and so his business has been. You may recall that when they accused him of a selfish motive – widening the market for his product – when he urged that our expenditures for armed strength be put into good roads, that he replied, "Now look here, the only reason for the existence of the Ford automobile is that we have bad roads in America. If there weren't any good roads the Ford car would have no competitors. Every time I speak for good roads I am helping my rivals."

From whatever attitude the articles to follow this one are viewed, they should be of interest, if only because of this fact – that they will strive to tell how Henry Ford works. For instance, how he arranges his machines, how he assembles his product, how he gets an unusual amount of work out of his payroll, how he preserves discipline, how he keeps his machines supplied with material, how he purchases, how he preserves quality in the face of a high-production record under unskilled labor, how he ships his product, how he sells the output, and how he advertises.

"GIVING THE MEN A SHARE": WHAT IT'S DOING FOR FORD

Harry Franklin Porter

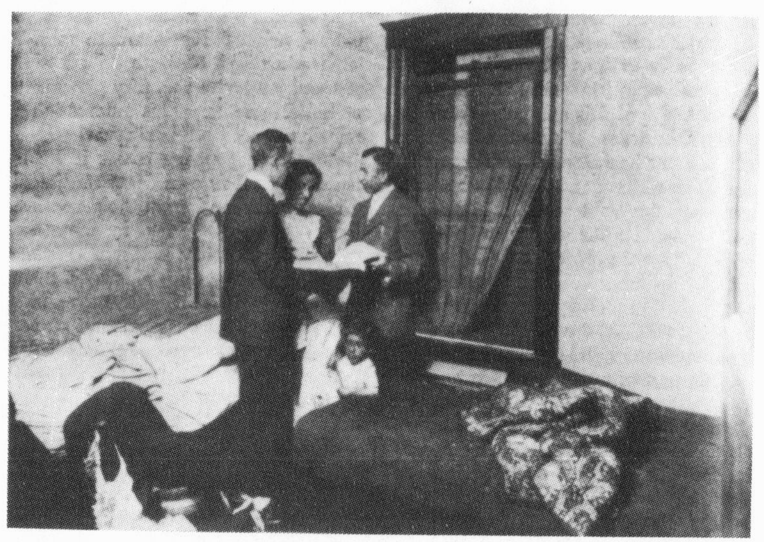

HELPING THE WORKER GET THE MOST OUT OF HIMSELF

It is the belief in the Ford plant that a workman who spends his out-of-shop hours in a dirty, ill-ventilated home is not able to do the best work. Accordingly, investigators are constantly studying conditions in the homes of Ford employees and suggesting improvements

"GIVING THE MEN A SHARE": WHAT IT'S DOING FOR FORD

By HARRY FRANKLIN PORTER *Illustrated with* PHOTOGRAPHS

MY FIRST introduction to the Ford plant and to Henry Ford was in the late spring of 1913. Although some of the most noteworthy developments in the short but eventful history of the Ford enterprise have taken place since that time, Henry Ford already was enjoying nation-wide distinction as a manufacturer. The annual convention of the National Association of Manufacturers was being held in Detroit and Mr. Ford was one of the guests at the banquet. When it became known that he was in the room, almost the sole topic of conversation at the outlying tables was Henry Ford and his methods.

A local manufacturer sat at my table and, as I personally was eager to learn more about Mr. Ford, I encouraged him to talk. He corroborated many of my previous impressions and filled in many interesting details. He was not, however, wholly laudatory in his remarks. As to the merit of Ford's mechanical methods he had nothing but praise. But as an employer of labor he criticized him. "He pays low wages and hires the cheapest class of help, mostly foreigners," was my table-mate's remark; "and," he added, "there is considerable feeling against him among Detroit manufacturers."

Just how much justice there was in this criticism I was unable to learn. I must confess that I was skeptical. I knew that one of the reasons for Ford's success was the extent to which he had carried the subdivision of labor, eliminating the necessity for any great skill on the part of many of his operatives. But I had also visited the plant and came away impressed with the excellence of the working conditions, the emphasis on good light, ventilation and sanitation, the provisions for safety, and the cheerful, busy atmosphere of the place. Therefore I was unwilling to believe that his methods as to men could be classed as retrogressive.

One of the officials of the Ford Motor Company, however, in a speech before the Indianapolis Chamber of Commerce, early in 1915, in leading up to an explanation of the Ford profit-sharing plan, made the following admission: "We, like other employers, had gone on for years, hiring men at the back door for as little as we could get them, putting them in the shop and making them work at the same job as long as they would stick, and not giving them an advance until we had to."

Then the tremendous wastes in this method of hiring and handling men began to dawn upon the Ford officials. They had not been exactly retrogressive in their labor policy, but they had unconsciously been following the line of least resistance. The result was that the number of five-day men, or "floaters," was very large. Some months it was necessary to hire new men to the extent of 55 per cent of the total payroll. When it is considered that the force comprised some seventeen thousand men, an idea can be had of the immensity of the task. The long employment line in front of the Ford plant had become one of the sights used to whet the curiosity of "rubber-neck" tourists.

Accordingly, a broad survey of the entire labor situation was undertaken. Other plants employing about the same number of men were visited, during the course of the investigation, but none with a better system was found. Nothing daunted the Ford heads determined to solve the problem in their own way. In the grading of employees they found great lack of uniformity. This matter had been largely in the hands of the foremen. As a result, operatives in different departments, and even in the same department, were doing virtually identical work, but were getting widely varying rates of pay.

AN UNUSUAL METHOD OF CLASSIFYING WORK

The number of different rates, moreover, was entirely too large. Therefore, as the first step, a comprehensive classification of skill was worked out. This was as original as it has been successful.

All the work was found to fall approximately into six different groups, or classes, of skill. Each of these divisions, or groups, in turn was subdivided into three groups—the beginners, those of average proficiency, and the highly proficient. An additional grade was further established in some of the divisions, that of service, to reward the proficient men who had been in the employ of the company continuously for two years or over. Rates of pay were fitted in accordance. These finally were boiled down to eight rates, as against some sixty rates that were originally in force.

In no case was a man's previous rate cut. On the contrary, rates on the whole were graded upward, and, when several rates were condensed into one, the new figure was slightly above even the highest of the ones it superseded. Rates from 52 to 58 cents, for instance, were condensed to 60 cents; from 46 cents to 50 cents, to 54 cents, and so on. The lowest rate per hour became 23 cents, for messengers and other miscel-

BEFORE–

Here is a typical row of workmen's houses as the Ford investigators commonly found them before any thought had been given to making the home life of employees more pleasant. Note the contrast between this picture and the one on the opposite page

laneous special labor; the highest 65 cents, for expert tool makers and foremen in the service for two years or over. This classification of skill became effective at the beginning of October, 1913.

Simultaneously the power of discharge was taken from the foremen and vested in a "court of appeal" working in connection with the employment office. Now, if a man fails to get along with his foreman he comes before this court, is carefully questioned, plainly talked to if at fault, and sent back to work in another department. Often it is a case of a "square peg in a round hole," and the man is shifted around until the work that he can do best is found. Of course, if a man shows, after two or three trials, that he hasn't it in him to make good, he is reluctantly let out.

The word "reluctantly" is used advisedly. It is difficult as things now are to get into the Ford organization, but once in it is perhaps more difficult to get out. The Ford Company wants its men to stay.

In addition to taking away the power to discharge from the foreman, systematic reviewing of the record of each workman was also inaugurated. If after the third pay day for a new man, for instance, no "raise slip" comes in, the foreman is sent for and asked why. If the man is entitled to promotion, but the matter simply has slipped the attention of the foreman, the latter is taken to task for his carelessness. He is also reproved if his failure to send in a slip is due to the man's inefficiency. He must not allow his department to be cumbered with a failure.

The toning-up effect of these measures can readily be appreciated. Men no longer were at a disadvantage because they happened to have incurred the dislike of their foremen. They were stimulated by the fact that the company was taking a personal interest in their welfare, and the new classification of skill remedied many injustices in the wage scale. The foremen, moreover, were aroused to a new sense of their responsibilities.

—AND AFTER

Paved streets, cheerful homes, and pleasant surroundings generally follow in the wake of the investigators who study living conditions among Ford employees. The houses pictured above are typical of the homes of a majority of Ford's employees

What the tangible results of the various measures inaugurated to insure more substantial justice to the individual workmen were are shown by the following figures:

	December, 1912	October, 1913
Five-day men......	3594	322
Men discharged.....	776	137
Men quitting.......	386	326
Men laid off........	4622	844
Total hired.........	5678	1789
Gain for the month..	856	954

The decrease in the number of five-day men, or "floaters," is particularly significant, since it indicates that permanency of the force was being achieved. The decrease in the number discharged also is noteworthy, and points to the success of the method of shifting men about until they make good, rather than letting them out on their first fall-down. The direct saving to the company through the greatly lessened employment expense was large, but the indirect saving through the greater efficiency of a reasonably permanent and contented working force, although more difficult to measure, was undoubtedly much larger. A decided decrease in the number tardy or absent was another result which had its financial compensations.

The striking fact is that Ford did not stop with these highly satisfactory results. The company was in a highly prosperous condition, sales exceeding all expectation. The men were receiving ten per cent more for nine hours' work than men in similar lines elsewhere in the vicinity were receiving for ten hours' work. In addition, they were getting an allowance of ten cents a day for carfare. Thus apparently there was no exciting cause to do anything further for them, beyond a thoroughly aroused desire of the Ford Motor Company to share its prosperity with its employees.

Many plans were considered. The idea of raising wages still further was dismissed. Various profit-sharing systems were investigated and they seemed unsatisfactory. So, as before, the Ford management went to work and devised an original plan. The details of this plan were given out early in January, 1914.

At one stroke the company reduced the hours from nine to eight, and added to every man's pay a share of the profits. The smallest amount to be received by any man 22 or more years old was five dollars a day. The minimum wage previously was $2.34 for a day of nine hours. All but ten per cent of the employees at once shared in the profits.

Only ten per cent of the men were under 22, and every one of them had a chance of showing himself entitled to five dollars per day. The factory had been working two shifts of nine hours each. This was changed to three shifts of eight hours each.

In order that the young man from 18 to 22 years of age might be entitled to a share in the profits, he was required to show himself sober, saving, steady, industrious, and to satisfy the superintendent and staff that his money would not be spent in extravagant living. Young men supporting families, widowed mothers, younger brothers and sisters – upon this condition – were to be treated like those over 22.

WHY ALL THE WORKERS DO NOT SHARE EQUALLY IN THE PROFITS

This has been called a profit-sharing plan. But it is quite unlike other plans of profit division, nor does it conform to any orthodox definition of profit sharing. The fact that the workman's share is predetermined, does not wait on the earnings of the company at the end of the year, and involves no investment by the men in the stock of the company, marks it as unusual. But what makes the plan absolutely unorthodox is the additional fact that those who earn the smallest wages get the largest share of the profits.

The plan has come in for much criticism on this score. When asked to give his reason Henry Ford, in his quaint, Lincolnesque manner, replied: "Well, it costs a sweeper just as much to raise his family properly as it does a mechanic or anybody else, doesn't it?"

It should be understood that the $5 a day is not a minimum wage. The rates of pay remain as before. But to each man's earnings is added a sufficient amount to bring his total reward to $5. A man who formerly received 23 cents an hour, or $2.07 for nine hours, now receives the same amount for eight hours: namely, $2.07 plus $2.93 as his share of the profits. The two sums are separately indicated on the pay envelope. The 44-cent-an-hour man receives $3.96 plus $1.04 for each day of eight hours.

Nor is $5 the maximum. Those who before were earning from 38 to 48 cents an hour, or the first-class skilled operatives and mechanics in the beginning grade, may share in the profits to the extent of bringing their total daily earnings up to $6; while those rated higher still, up to where the salary class begins, may receive as much as $7 a day. The 54-cent-an-hour man's share of the profits at that is only $2.14, as against $2.93 for the man rated lowest. Salaried men do not share, but are taken care of separately through a bonus plan which is equivalent.

At first the only ones barred from participation in the profits were the young men under 22, who had only themselves to support. Later it was found expedient to include in the non-participants all new men until they have been on the payroll for six months. The chief reason for this change, which took effect in October, 1914, was to discourage men in other plants from quitting their jobs in order to get the higher earnings possible in the Ford plant. But it also has its virtue as a means of testing the intentions of newcomers. If they stick it out six months at ordinary wages they usually have the necessary qualities to make them permanent members of the force. Again, it gives the company ample time to check up on their living habits and financial status, and – if these are undesirable – to improve them in the mean-

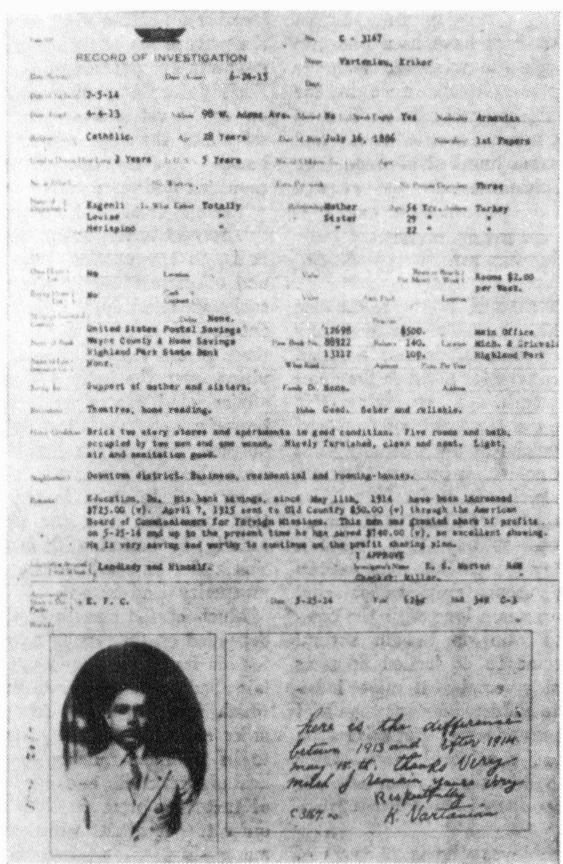

RECORD OF INVESTIGATION

C - 3167

Vartanian, Erikor

6-26-15

3-5-14

4-6-13 — 90 W. Adams Ave. — No — Yes — Armenian

Catholic — 28 Years — July 16, 1886 — 1st Papers

3 Years — 5 Years

Three

Eugenie — Totally — Mother — 54 Yrs. — Turkey
Louise — " — Sister — 29 " — "
Herispime — " — " — 22 " — "

No — Rooms $2.00 per Week.

No

None.

United States Postal Savings — 12698 — $500. — Main Office
Wayne County & Home Savings — 88922 — 140. — Mich. & Griswold
Highland Park State Bank — 13117 — 100. — Highland Park
None.

Support of mother and sisters. — None.

Theatres, home reading. — Good. Sober and reliable.

Brick two story stores and apartments in good condition. Five rooms and bath, occupied by two men and one woman. Nicely furnished, clean and neat. Light, air and sanitation good.

Downtown district. Business, residential and rooming-houses.

Education, No. His bank savings, since May 11th, 1914 have been increased $723.00 (v). April 7, 1915 sent to Old Country $30.00 (v) through the American Board of Commissioners for Foreign Missions. This man was granted share of profits on 5-25-14 and up to the present time he has saved $740.00 (v), an excellent showing. He is very saving and worthy to continue on the profit sharing plan.

I APPROVE

Landlady and Himself. — E. S. Morton — Miller.

E. F. C. — 5-25-14

Respectfully
K. Vartanian

WHAT FORD KNOWS ABOUT HIS MEN

A report sheet like this is made out for each employee in the Ford plant. In order to share in the profits, employees must receive a "clean bill of health" from the investigators on the various points shown above

time until they come up to the Ford standards, so that there will be no doubt of the man's ability to qualify for participation in the profits at the end of the six months.

Further, in order to protect other plants, and to discourage the in-drift of men from other cities, the Ford Motor Company now will entertain as applicants only those actually out of employment and who have been bona fide residents of Detroit, or the vicinity, for at least six months.

At first the plan of profit division applied only to the shops. It has since been extended to include the office force as well. The Ford branches and assembly plants are on the same basis; and in both the Ford Canadian and English plants similar plans have been put into effect, although the minimum is lower there, owing to the difference in the American and British wage scales. Women in the factory who are breadwinners – and there are several hundred of them – are treated precisely as men.

HOW THE WOMEN WORKERS ARE PAID

Women as a class, however, are not profit sharers. Instead, the company gave them a substantial increase in wages. The minimum now for a girl in the office is $65 a month. In explaining this difference in the treatment of men and women, an official of the company said: "Women do not share because they are not, as a rule, heads of families. Also women, as a rule, are likely to throw up their positions at any time, without notice, for any reason that may happen to influence them, even temporarily. Few of them remain long with the company. Those who do remain several years, and come to be looked upon as reliable, steady employees, not infrequently make sudden announcements of their marriages and leave. For this reason they are not considered such stable economic factors as men. An advance in pay is considered more appropriate for them."

For the employee who is 22 years of age, and who has been on the payroll six months or longer, the sole disbarment condition is persistence in habits of life which fall short of the standard the Ford Motor Company believes essential in a decent, self-respecting American workman. While what a man *is* on the outside is reflected to a greater or less extent in his demeanor and the quality of his workmanship, the only practical way in which the company could check up in this respect was by personal visits to the homes.

So without pausing to debate the fine-spun, theoretical aspects of the act, as to whether an extension of supervision over the private life of their workers was unwarrantably paternalistic or not, the Ford Motor Company instituted a follow-up or "investigation" department and set about the huge task of visiting the homes of every one of its seventeen thousand and more employees.

The efforts of the Ford organization in this respect have borne remarkable fruit. It is, in my opinion, most practicable and effective social welfare work. It is espionage in a way, but of a totally different sort than ordinarily implied by this term. Ford exercises the closest supervision over the home life and financial affairs of his workmen. He does it, however, openly and frankly and for the purpose, not of taking something away from them or persecuting them, but in order to help them in the most practical way one man can help another: namely, by bettering his financial condition and then teaching him how to use prosperity to advantage.

Much of the success of the plan has depended on the type of men Ford chose for his investigators. Men's private affairs had to be pried into, facts secured which in many cases required a high order of detective ability, and they had to be obtained quickly. Persistence, a deal of shrewdness, and an infinite amount of tact thus were requisite qualities in order to get results with a minimum of antagonism. Men, the slaves of all manner of bad habits, the victims of new-world vices and old-world standards of living, had to be made to see the worth-while side of manly attributes and decent, clean home conditions.

Definite, measurable results are plentiful. Of the many families reunited; the drug and liquor addicts reformed; the criminally inclined who have been reclaimed; the debt-burdened families relieved; of the hundreds of children clothed and fed decently for perhaps the first time; the thousands of homes cleaned up and made livable; of the eleven or twelve thousand families that have been moved from the slums and undesirable, congested locations to outlying suburbs and country districts, most of them into nice little cottages of their own; of the tremendous increase in savings deposits, insurance carried, and payments on land and home contracts – of these and other concrete results of the Ford efforts in behalf of their workers, it would be possible to write in great detail. Perhaps the most striking evidence, however, was the way in which the investigators were received in the homes.

Henry Ford has been extremely interested in the foreign-born workmen, of whom there are some 52 nationalities comprising in number more than half his force. He feels he must shoulder his part of the burden of making them feel at home here, and of preparing them for speedy assimilation into our national life.

The very fact, however, that so many of the Ford employees were foreign born and non-English speaking, greatly complicated – at the start – the administration of the profit-sharing plan, and particularly the labor of the investigators. It was difficult in the first place to get them to understand the conditions. Many were the curious and incorrect impressions which it took a long time to eradicate. One idea, for instance, was that all a man had to do to qualify for a share in the profits was to get married. Immediately, men who were wifeless took steps to remedy the deficiency, fairly or otherwise. Some hastily married, others persuaded or hired women friends or relatives to act as their wives, still others faked marriage certificates, asserting their wives were on the other side of the water. All these tangles had to be patiently straightened out, the men made to see the error of misrepresenting the facts and the unwisdom of precipitous matrimony.

Another impression was to the effect that if a man owned real estate he would get the profits, and for a time some real estate men reaped a harvest. By a singular coincidence, one man bought real estate on such an assurance and the very next day he went on the profit payroll. The news, of course, spread rapidly. As a result that particular real estate man signed up many advantageous contracts the next few days. Then the Ford officials got wind of the affair and through the legal department forced the real estate man to release every Ford employee unfairly inveigled into contracts.

This and similar experiences led the company to undertake supervision of the men's legal affairs. A representative of the legal department now makes his headquarters in the employment department and the men are strongly urged, before entering into any real estate deals, to confer with him.

HOW THE COMPANY LOOKS OUT FOR THE INTERESTS OF ITS EMPLOYEES

Other special purchases are supervised similarly. Many of the men were found to be debt ridden with instalment purchases. So the company frankly took up the matter with the various suppliers of household luxuries and got them to agree not to sign up a contract with a Ford employee until they had first conferred with the company and ascertained his ability to make good on his payments. The evil of garnishees has been almost eliminated by similar cooperation between local merchants and the company. Before instituting legal proceedings the merchants are urged to take up the matter with the Ford officials, who usually are able to make some arrangement for the resumption of payments. To rid themselves as promptly as possible of all indebtedness, and to guard against becoming reincumbered, is one of the lessons which the company, through its sociological department, endeavors constantly to hammer home to the workmen.

In passing, it should be mentioned that many of the little plans devised by the men to make themselves appear qualified for promotion when they really are not, such as the falsification of marriage certificates, succeeded temporarily. In practically every case, however, the Ford investigators eventually penetrated these deceits. The company did not discharge the men so caught. If they did not voluntarily leave they were given a wholesome talking to about the need for truth telling on all occasions, and the lesson was made concrete by compelling them to pay back every penny falsely obtained. If a man refused to stay and pay the company took the matter to court and invariably secured the decision.

The large proportion of non-English speaking employees greatly hampered the investigators, for it required them to work through interpreters. Men competent to act as interpreters were hard to find.

HOW EDUCATIONAL WORK IN THE FORD PLANT IMPROVES PROFITS

The difficulties with men who could not speak, read nor write English, however, soon led the company to organize for instruction in English. This was early in 1914. An experienced educator was called in. Under his energetic leadership, with a teaching staff of volunteers drawn mostly from the ranks of foremen, a class of over a thousand was graduated at the end of 37 weeks. At the present time approximately sixteen hundred men are receiving instruction. Two lessons a week are given. Attendance is compulsory for those who have registered.

Undertaken solely out of interest in the men, this educational work nevertheless has proved itself extremely profitable to the Ford company. There has been, for one thing, a measurable decrease in accidents, as most of the personal injury cases were formerly among foreigners, whose lack of comprehension of the language often prevented them from learning the safety precautions thoroughly. Many also were hurt because when told to "look out," they did not understand, and actually got in the way of danger instead of out of its reach. Their efficiency as workers has also increased, due to their growing feeling for the organization and the additional knowledge they have been able to pick up through understanding English. Supervision, moreover, has been lessened. Not the least of the benefits has come through the different attitude induced in the foremen by their volunteer work as teachers.

If the teaching of English has had its measurable financial compensations to the Ford Company, the profit-sharing plan as a whole has been even more productive. That it would prove extremely profitable in a dollars-and-cents way at no time entered as an element in the calculations.

In fact, I have it on the authority of one of the high officials of the company that "the Ford Company had no desire to experiment in the direction of increasing the efficiency of its employees, as measured in terms of individual work and daily output."

Within a very short time after the inauguration of the plan there was a voluntary increase of from fifteen to twenty per cent, in spite of the fact that each man worked one hour less. On the fourth of February, 1913, with 16,000 men working ten hours a day, the company made and shipped 16,000 units of its product. The same month, one year later, after the new plan had been in effect a little over a month, with 15,800 men working eight hours a day, it made and shipped 26,000 units. At the present time, with approximately 18,000 workers, it is producing at a rate of over 40,000 units a month.

Some of this gain, it is true, has come about through improved methods, but much of it has been due to the increased interest, loyalty and efficiency of the force. Working less hours a day, the men are able to sustain a higher rate of output each hour. Reasonably certain of the permanency of their employment and happy in the knowledge that they are gaining on the rising cost of living, they are rid of fear and worry.

FOUR BIG LESSONS FROM FORD'S FACTORY

Harry Franklin Porter

TESTING AS YOU GO ALONG

Each assembly unit of the Ford product is tested separately, so that when the car is completely assembled it must run perfectly. Here, in the foreground, is a workman testing the differential

FOUR BIG LESSONS FROM FORD'S FACTORY

The huge output of the Ford Motor Company permits the use of some special methods and machines that would be impracticable in smaller concerns. On the other hand, just because of its size, the company has had to give careful attention to the study of most problems that are common to all plants, large and small alike. This article describes these latter plans – four general principles so fundamentally important that you can almost surely apply them with profit in your plant, though it occupy but the space of a single floor in a loft building. You'll no doubt find it particularly well worth your while to study these plans now, when the war makes it important for every concern to secure the greatest output with the least possible waste of materials and human effort

By HARRY FRANKLIN PORTER — *Illustrated with* PHOTOGRAPHS

CONSIDERING the rapid changes in the motor-car industry, it is surprising that Henry Ford has with the years felt it necessary to change the design of his product so little. While each year sees a few changes, mostly refinements in details that reduce cost without impairing the quality, the essential part of the product – the motor and driving mechanism – has not been altered one iota in five years.

In view of the volume of Ford production, think what this means! If any other piece of machinery has ever been manufactured in consecutive, unchanged form into the millions, I have yet to hear of it. Having found a motor that so far as they could determine was perfect, the designers left it alone. Barring revolutionary developments in motor-vehicle drive, it is likely to remain unchanged indefinitely.

To this fact is due very largely the astonishing degree of standardization and specialization you find in the Ford plant. The entire organization operates with almost the mechanical precision of an automatic screw-machine or a multiple web-perfected printing press.

Assured of a practically unlimited run on the one model, the Ford engineers and superintendents have had a free hand in selecting and developing machinery, special tools, dies, methods, and men. Volume of production enabled them to specialize to a greater extent than the average factory perhaps, but without rigid standardization of design this specialization would have served only to make the manufacturing problem the more unwieldy.

SOME OF THE ADVANTAGES OF A STANDARD DESIGN

Nothing is quite so demoralizing to the smooth and economical operation of a factory as incessant changes in design. Even small changes at the beginning of a season occasion much confusion for weeks or months; meanwhile, production is curtailed and costs go skyward. When these changes are incessant, as they are in many plants, due to the lack of concentration and skill on the part of the designers or to the whims of the management, the work of standardizing machines or methods obviously cannot progress so very far.

Not only is it impossible to get up much organization momentum, but no one has the heart definitely to standardize any one operation; nor does the management, for its part, feel justified ordinarily in financing many far-reaching improvements. The result is a double loss – that directly chargeable to the changes themselves, such as prematurely obsolete equipment and the loss of organization momentum; and the higher cost of operating more or less continuously under half-developed standards.

This, then, is Ford's great lesson for other manufacturers – let standardization begin with the design of the product itself. Ford believes in spending plenty of time to perfect the model in the first place. Thereafter, he tolerates no changes that are not fully justified by economic considerations.

The effect on the Ford organization of minor changes in the product when cast iron and pressed steel were substituted for aluminum and brass in certain parts, and when crown fenders and a streamline hood were adopted to improve the appearance of the finished product, doubly emphasizes the disadvantage of design changes. The first month saw production curtailed fully fifty per cent; and it was nearly three months before the entire organization could be geared up for the stipulated work. Meanwhile, orders piled up and the sales force was in despair.

Financially the loss ran into the thousands – a loss which it may take years of uninterrupted production to wipe out. Yet the changes were no doubt fully justified. Changes must come. Only a stubborn and shortsighted manager will set his face against any and all changes. But by proper management it is usually possibly greatly to lengthen the interval between changes. This is the Ford policy and it is one that seems well worthy of emulation.

Summed up, the advantages of a standardized design – over a long period at any rate – are as follows:

1. The shop can calculate its requirements far in advance.

2. Special equipment and tools can be developed practically unhampered.

3. Methods of work and of handling materials can be thoroughly standardized.

4. Supervision and inspection through repeated exercise become expert. This

makes for more uniform quality and reduces the percentage of waste.

5. Operators, engaged regularly on repetitive work, become highly proficient. The entire organization, in fact, becomes a body of specialized experts.

6. Tool designers and methods engineers can devote their attention to changes in equipment and methods that will effect further cost reductions or increase the output per unit of floor space or per man.

7. The purchasing department can anticipate the requirements for raw materials, not only months but even years in advance, and can take the fullest advantage of business and market conditions.

8. The management is freed of perhaps its biggest source of worry.

9. Manufacturing expense, costs, and profits can be prefigured with almost uncanny precision.

Not slow have the Ford engineers and superintendents been to make the fullest use of these advantages afforded by standardization of design.

In every department specialized equipment and specialized methods of doing work are found, that give the impression of having been devised in disregard of temporary considerations, and with only the utmost economy of operation in view.

Many of the special machines, it should be said, would not be justified save for the unprecedented scale of operation. Take the great semi-automatic milling machine for front axles costing thousands of dollars; perhaps only Ford has the output to justify such machines. So it is with his semi-automatic multiple gear-cutting machines and many others.

On the other hand, Ford has developed many types of special machines or specialized uses of standard machines, which are perfectly usable in much smaller

KEEPING THE PACE STEADY

Work in process is constantly moving, and each workman performs one operation as the material passes him. Here, for example, are seats passing slowly down the assembly room on a chain conveyor

AN EASY WAY TO LIFT

Here is another use for a chain conveyor. This one does away with the need for an elevator at one point, hoisting the automobile bodies up an incline for temporary storage on the fourth floor

shops. His wide adoption of standard punch and arbor presses and broaching machines, for instance, contains suggestions for every manufacturer in metal.

But it is his progressive system of assembling that seems to be most generally applicable, and this system I find is being rapidly introduced not only in most motor vehicle factories, but in many other lines. It has made its way into the stove industry and the woodworking industry. The equipment investment is comparatively light and in a small factory standard production can be handled to advantage by this method.

"Keep the product on the move" has for many years been recognized as a cardinal principle of economical factory operation. In recognition of this principle, conveyors of various types have in recent years come into wide use in all lines of industry.

WHY FORD DOES NOT NEED MANY STORE ROOMS FOR MATERIALS

Ford in this respect is well towards the head of the procession. Material seldom is at rest in his plant; when it isn't being processed it is rolling down a chute on a conveyor of some kind for the next operation. Only in passing from the primary shops – the foundry and the forge – to rough-piece store rooms or to the machine shop, and hence to the various assemblies, does it ever travel in lots. Elsewhere the pieces move singly in an unending stream, from one operation to the next.

It was but natural, therefore, that a shop where production already was so fluid should come to a system of progressive assembling. A major part – an axle or a cyliner block – is placed on a conveyor whose pace is carefully regulated to permit the various subsequent operations to be performed as the piece with its accretions passes by. One man may only screw on a nut or two. He may have to move two or three feet while doing this; seldom more. The initial attendant – the man who feeds the chain – therefore has the regularity of production entirely under his control, and he is especially selected and paid to see that the line is an unbroken procession.

Often men are especially charged with the duty of keeping the head of the line, and other points along the way where additional parts are added, supplied with material. In many cases these deliveries are made by conveyor or chute, which in turn are fed continuously. Where necessary, stocks of parts are accumulated at feeding points. A special factory department, known as the stock-chasing department, is charged with the duty of keeping tab on these stocks and seeing that delays due to shortages of material do not occur.

Clerks or messengers bring in hourly reports of production in the various departments for the general superintendent's office. There the reports are at once posted to a large blackboard, and thus the superintendents can see at a glance just how things are running. The superintendent's assistant is especially charged to watch this board, and if he notices a tendency to slow up at any point he at once calls attention to it.

Production must be kept in balance. The supply of all materials needed to keep the producer busy must be perfect. Lapses in either of these respects that might not be noticed in a less thoroughly standardized and specialized shop, would if given any leeway here cause untold havoc. Thorough standardization in one department, therefore, entails equally thorough standardization in all other inter-dependent departments.

Castings are molded, the upholstery is made, and the bodies are trimmed, painted and finally fitted on the progressive or continuous-work principle. Everything possible is done while the material is in motion.

Perhaps the most interesting of the non-assembly operations is the molding of the cylinder blocks. This is done on an endless conveyor. On one side the molds are being prepared. At one end

BRINGING THE JOB TO THE MAN

This man is doing a bit of under-the-car assembly work. The car is routed over the pit in which he stands, so that it is not necessary for him to move more than a few steps in order to complete his task. The cars come to him in a steady procession

they are poured, at the other end they are picked up one by one with a pneumatic hoisting carriage tended by one man. The hoisting carriage first turns the mold over, dumping the casting, and then deposits the flask and pattern – all semi-automatically. The parts of the mold are at once sorted and delivered by helpers to various points along the line, where they go to build up new molds. The castings, dumped while still red hot, are allowed to remain in the sand until cool. But even this rest has a purpose. They anneal as they cool, thus making unnecessary the usual special annealing operation.

Pistons, piston rings, valve heads, crank cases and other parts of gray iron are molded and cast in much the same fashion. The molds are not in all cases built up in motion, but they are poured while in motion. The molds go to meet the pourer on one side; and on the other side large vessels of molten iron – direct from one of the cupolas, and traveling on a monorail – come to meet him at the head of the line. Hooks suspended from a monorail concentric with the conveyor hold his pot as he moves from mold to mold, so that he need never bear the entire weight of a full pot more than a few feet.

Contrast this arrangement with that found in a good many foundries, where the molds are widely scattered and the pourer must sometimes run with his pot a hundred feet or more. Not only is the Ford method capable of yielding an immensely greater tonnage per unit of floor space, but it is much less arduous and safer. Any foundry making quantities of uniform pieces could apply the same principle.

Equipment obviously sets the pace in the Ford shops. That is why Ford needs no highly refined method of wage payment to furnish an incentive for high output. The men must very nearly do a standard day's production whether they wish to or not. And because they are well paid and share in the profits – because, too, working conditions are good and the hours of work are short – the average Ford employee, like Barkus, is usually quite "willin'." Nor is the pace strenuous. The men are kept reasonably busy, but no one in my observation appeared to be rushed.

Even in operations where mechanical pace setting is impossible, Ford still achieves the effect of a piece system without paying by the piece. Perhaps one of the best examples of how he does this is found in the top department.

ONE WAY OF GETTING THE WORK THROUGH FASTER

Here the operators who are engaged in stitching together the top material are seated at parallel benches. The material starts at the back row and works toward the front. There are five rows of benches in all. By having a little more capacity on the rear row than on the one in front of it, and again on the second a slight excess over the third, and so on, the work has a tendency to pile up on the succeeding rows. A sporting instinct comes into play, for the operators behind are constantly, with a little handicap, striving to overwhelm those immediately in front; while those in front are striving as constantly not only to crowd the fellows in front of them but to keep from being crowded by the chaps behind.

To stir up competition among the operators in any one row of benches, where all are doing identically the same operation, production boards are maintained at the end of each row. Here the output of each man is posted hourly, and the records of those who equal or better the quota set are written down in colored crayon. A record is kept of the "color men," and as supervisors or inspectors are needed, they are selected from this roll.

I have been in many garment factories. Never have I seen bench machine operators, under any system of wage-payment, more industrious or more thoroughly imbued with the spirit of individual and group effort. This demonstrates the truth of the statement credited to the late Frederick W. Taylor that surprising results can be had under daywork if conditions are standardized and production rests upon a basis of exact knowledge. Mr. Taylor is said to have criticized unsparingly the Ford plan of a five dollar minimum wage for each man, regardless of his output. But subsequently, learning how Ford regulated his production, he revoked his criticism. There is mighty little chance for a shirker to persist in the Ford plant, even though the entire force is paid on a daywork basis.

In the assembly lines, for instance, if a man for any reason, willful or otherwise, is unable to hold up his end, the fact is at once apparent to the supervisor and this particular man must immediately give way to another. He is not dismissed for failing to make good, but is given ample opportunity to demonstrate his ability elsewhere. Only if he fails after repeated trials is he "fired." And this is necessary in very, very few instances.

Men are also encouraged to use either hand with equal facility and to employ both hands simultaneously. On assembly benches, for instance, where the operators are lined up opposite each other, they are shifted periodically from one side to the other in order to accustom them to work either way. This system is not only an assurance against emergency vacancies, but in many instances throughout the shops it enables a man to accomplish again as much work. From the worker's viewpoint, this dual facility increases his skill and is an assurance of continued employment in case a hand or an arm should be lost.

This is but another example of the Ford guiding principle of getting the most out of every resource. Floor space is utilized to a degree seldom seen in

THERE'S NO NEED FOR LIFTING HERE

These multiple drills are placed side by side so that the castings can pass from one to the other with least lifting. Each set of drills does just its own share of the work, thus making it unnecessary to reset drills frequently

American factories. Machines are not set down haphazard. Their location with respect to other machines is carefully studied, and they are placed not only so as to save space, but also to enable the passing of work practically from hand to hand. Where two machines performing successive operations on a piece can not be placed so close together, or where the pieces are too heavy to be handled by hand, chutes or inclines are provided. No operator needs to leave his machine either to deliver work to the man ahead or to get it from the man behind.

Overhead space, as well as floor space, serves a definite purpose. The toilets, for example, instead of occupying valuable floor space, are located here and there throughout the shop on mezzanines, below which are the tool and supply storages. Progressive drying ovens are similarly located, when the room height permits it.

Overhead, too, is the main material transportation system – a monorail which covers all parts of the machine shop and links it with the supplying departments. If trucking were confined to the floors, the shop would be hopelessly congested most of the time, or else considerably more floor space would have to be sacrificed for trucking aisles.

Not even the roof has escaped use. The entire roof of the four-story building to the rear of the administration building is the cooling area for the power house condensers; while the roof of the new six-story building to the rear of the machine and assembly shops is covered with the main ducts of the air-conditioning system. The outlet branches of this air-conditioning system, by the way, run down through the center of the building's interior supports.

Another question: does Ford also use his buildings to the utmost from sun to sun? Yes and no. Some departments operate three shifts, many two, a few only one. It is the intention, as soon as the space can be provided, to discontinue 24-hour continuous operations entirely.

The third shift, starting at midnight, has not proved a success. Its production is not equal to that of the other shifts and the men do not seem to stand up well under it. It will be abandoned, even though some overhead cost might be saved by continuing and extending it.

AVOIDING INTERRUPTIONS IN THE FACTORY

Uninterrupted production presupposes not only evenly balanced departments and nicely timed material deliveries, but also a system of maintenance which assures the steady operation of each machine at its best speed. Here, with Ford, money and pains are no object. A large and able corps of oilers, electricians, tool conditioners, tool setters, and tool and machine supervisors is on duty constantly.

Plenty of spare cutting tools are kept on hand and special supervisors patrol the floor, watching for the first sign that a tool is failing to hold the pace or produce the requisite quality. Without waiting for an offending tool to get worse, the supervisor immediately stops the machine and inserts a fresh tool. The operators, with minor exceptions, are relieved of responsibility.

What about the control exercised over quality? Is everything sacrificed for volume of output? By no means. Both the safety engineer and the quality boss have authority to arrest production at any point where they observe conditions that menace either safety or quality; and the conditions must be corrected before the machine can be used again for production.

Inspection, like supervision and labor itself, is finely specialized. The inspection department is, in fact, an entire organization by itself. At the head, occupying an office, is a chief inspector, who is responsible to the works manager and the chief engineer. Directly responsible to him are the general department inspectors. Inspection in the entire machine shop, for example, is in charge of one man. Under him are several assistant chief inspectors, each responsible for a section of the shop. Under these men, again, are the operational inspectors, whose stations in all departments are close to the production they check on. The inspection is to all intents and purposes an integral part in the sequence of productive operations.

The inspectors are served by truckers whose business it is to remove and deliver to the proper place pieces thrown out. Many pieces simply have to be returned for a little more processing. Those flatly rejected are taken to a central point where a special inspector gives them attention and decides their final destination – whether they can be rescued without too great expense, or whether they are fit only for the scrap pile. Even the scrap pile is afterward intensively mined, and many dollars' worth of material recovered from it – but that is a story by itself. Then there are floor inspectors whose duty it is to check up the first piece on each set-up, and every so many pieces thereafter.

Entering material is inspected, before it is definitely accepted, in a similar thoroughgoing fashion. Nothing that is not strictly according to specifications is allowed to join the stream of production. Ford does not stop even here, for sometimes he sends his inspectors to the supplier's factory to pass on the goods before they are even shipped. More than that, he frequently sends his chief receiving inspectors to a supplier's plant to help the latter correct some fault that is causing too heavy a percentage of rejections. Ford considers that this is not only a loss to the supplier, but it might occasion shortages of important material and thus hold up his own production.

WHAT A NEW SYSTEM OF MANAGEMENT DID FOR US

John S. Runnells

JOHN S. RUNNELLS

THE President of the Pullman Company is one of that group of brilliant lawyers – E. H. Gary, R. S. Lovett, Theodore P. Shonts, *et al.* – who entered American business as legal advisers and have succeeded to the executive direction of great enterprises. On page 116 Mr. Runnells begins a notable series of articles on the "common-sense system of management" which has worked wonders at Pullman

SYSTEM
THE MAGAZINE OF BUSINESS

VOLUME XXIX FEBRUARY, 1916 NUMBER 2

What a *New System* of Management Did for Us

The President of the Pullman Company tells how a combination of the Taylor system with the company's own policies and methods effected "astonishing results"

THIS is the story of the making-over of a great industry forty-five years after it started. It is told by the executive who is chiefly responsible for the change.

Two factors brought about the reorganization – a Condition and an Idea.

The Condition grew out of the practicability of securing greater safety in travel. The public wanted steel cars – particularly that public which paid extra fares to travel in Pullman comfort, and the Pullman Company after forty years of building wooden "sleepers," faced the necessity of adopting a new raw material and changing over its factory to a steel-working plant.

The Idea was a parallel development. When the change began, John S. Runnells, president of the company, tried to hire F. W. Taylor to reorganize the Pullman works. Taylor refused because so great a task would mean the giving up of his other undertakings. He offered his counsel free; but a visit to his pet factory in Philadelphia, with its hundred workmen, made the Taylor system seem inapplicable to the huge car shops unless it could be worked out on a new scale by the great engineer himself.

HOW the Condition and the Idea finally came together in "a definite plan of common-sense management," Mr. Runnells tells in the series of articles which he introduces in the pages following. It is not the Taylor system, though the inquiry with which it began was prompted by Mr. Taylor's achievements and the reorganization has been assisted in many important phases by one of the engineers most closely associated with Mr. Taylor in his work. Some parts of this "common-sense system" are one hundred per cent Taylor: others which will be described may run counter to accepted Taylor practice. But all are grounded on the basic idea of finding the one right material and handling it in the one right way.

Despite the size of the car works, the Pullman idea can be applied in the small factory. Indeed, the Pullman plant is an assemblage of small factories grouped about a large-scale fabricating and erecting plant. A paint shop, repair shop, brass foundry, machine shop, toolmaking departments and many other individual units have had to solve production problems very similar both in kind and scale to those which the average manufacturer encounters every day.

SELDOM, however, has SYSTEM found an executive of Mr. Runnells' caliber willing to give so freely of his time and knowledge in the preparation of a series of authoritative articles. To spare Mr. Runnells all unnecessary labor, Mr. Joseph Husband, whose new book "America at Work" stamps him as a man of business vision and understanding, was commissioned to study the Pullman system of management – to gather and arrange the significant materials for Mr. Runnells' consideration – and to transcribe the story and the facts as only Mr. Runnells could define and interpret them. The following article is substantially as narrated by Mr. Runnells in a recent interview with Mr. Husband.

BY JOHN S. RUNNELLS *Transcribed by* JOSEPH HUSBAND

IN THE year 1880, George M. Pullman established a manufacturing community and an extensive plant for the manufacture of the company's product, on a deserted stretch of prairie near Chicago, which now, a part of the greater city, still bears his name.

It had been Mr. Pullman's hope for a long time to found a model industrial community, and when the rumor of his intention became current, there was great speculation as to the site he would select.

Pullman, in 1880, was prairie, but in two years the transformation was completed, and a town had risen complete in every detail, a great industrial community, with shops, houses, churches, parks, schools, a library, and a theatre – a model town, perfect in every detail, planned by a single mind. Ten thousand was its population.

Beneath this perfect expression of the physical need of a great industrial community lay the altruistic purpose of the founder. Pullman was built on the theory that workmen comfortably housed, with proper facilities for the comfort and recreation of themselves and their families, would be better workmen.

The theory was correct. Although the strike of 1894 wounded the heart of the founder, and for a time made him doubt his faith, it was not an expression of the men themselves – but a strike inspired by outside influence.

A few years thereafter, as the result of litigation which ended in a decision that the company could not legally own the town of Pullman, the company disposed of its ownership and control. As a matter of fact, the houses were sold almost entirely to workmen in the company's employ under such conditions as to time and mode of payment, that they were able to buy them. The town is now practically entirely owned by them.

The deep interest of the officers of the company in this interesting community problem, as well as their interest in the increase of the efficiency of the great organization, through which wages might be bettered and at the same time savings made for the company, led but a short time ago to the preliminary steps which soon pointed the way to a definite plan of common-sense management.

One of the first steps was naturally a careful investigation of prevailing conditions. Within a period of five years a fundamental change, such as was making over many American manufacturing concerns at that time, had taken place at Pullman. It had become a steel-working plant instead of a wood-working plant. At first all the cars were of wood; now they are made of steel. A wood-working plant employs many carpenters and other workers who do not use heavy machinery in accomplishing their tasks. A steel-working plant requires a large amount of heavy machinery and an increased centralization naturally results from the use of this machinery. It is the old story that always grows out of an extensive use of heavy machines in place of more or less detached tasks accomplished by hand.

This primary investigation, covering a period of several months, was most thoroughly and successfully performed by a member of my office force, who soon proved himself fully equal to the difficult task that had been given to him. To his very efficient work in this connection many of the improvements which have followed are largely due.

His first reports were naturally limited, due chiefly to the vastness of the field and the lack of data to work with, but a number of his recommendations challenged immediate attention.

Among the suggestions received from our own men was one regarding a checking system, which was soon after adopted. Short as the period was in which it was given trial, the results were so amazing that it was apparent wisdom to continue it and develop it along widening lines.

Such was the beginning and this checking system for piece-work was inaugurated as almost our first step in establishing the new system of management. Before this checking plan was put in force a "job" would be given out to a "gang" of any number of men the foremen guessed that the work would require. The men would then divide up the work among themselves.

WHAT THE CHECKING SYSTEM ACCOMPLISHED FIRST OF ALL

It was a very crude way and resulted in tremendous time wastes. The first thing that came out of the checking system was the practical elimination of this evil together with the discovery that some men under the old system – or lack of system – had been inadequately paid, and that some were over paid. The result of the checking was an equalization of the pay.

It is interesting at this point, to recall that a number of years before this investigation, my attention was called by my predecessor, Mr. Robert T. Lincoln, to an article on this very subject of more systematic management by Frederick W.

PLATFORM *for* THE "SALVAGE"

***THIS** platform was built for "salvaged" tools when the Pullman Company decided to abandon the methods under which, to use the words of Mr. Runnells, "every workman got all the tools he wanted, as many duplicates as he could, in addition, and stowed them away"*

Taylor, who up to then was unknown to me – an article which I naturally read with the greatest interest.

In some measure, as the result of this article, and the impression created by it on our directors, I had the pleasure of meeting Mr. Taylor a short time later in Philadelphia, and laying our problem before him.

The thing that struck Mr. Taylor most forcibly was the fact that Pullman was by far the biggest plant the officials of which had ever investigated his system. But what was more remarkable, was the attitude of the man, for although we would gladly have acquired his services at a good compensation, he preferred to

regard his work as a philanthropy; offering freely his advice and recommendations, but declining absolutely to restrict his work to one large concern, in his consideration of the universal need for his services. He said he would give his time without expense to the general cause, but that he did not want to limit himself to any one plant.

During my visit he took me to see a small plant, which was enjoying the complete system he had devised, but notwithstanding the fact that the system had brought back this particular company

ON TOP *of* THE PLATFORM

HERE are some of the "salvaged" tools piled on top of the platform shown in the illustration on the opposite page. Thousands of dollars' worth of tools were brought together for orderly issuance by the establishment of the cent: al tool room to which this platform is an adjunct

literally from the dead and made it a profit-making concern, it seemed impractical to consider it for Pullman in

HOW THE WORK IS DIRECTED

IN this room the work of a part of the plant – or it might be a small independent plant, of course – is mapped out. The two men are receiving instructions, which are marked with a time stamp. The boards are arranged by machines, and provide for instructions covering three jobs – the one in hand, the one next ahead, and even the second ahead

its entirety. Although the system unquestionably contained many things of value, Pullman was too big a plant for its immediate and complete adoption.

As the result of this meeting, arrangements were made with one of Mr. Taylor's assistants, Carl G. Barth, who was very highly recommended by Mr. Taylor, and whose recommendations I have since found to have been most amply justified, to devote a part of his time to the company's interests, and with his assistance, and the information already obtained from our own investigations, a series of ideas were selected to meet the individual requirements of the Pullman Company. It is sufficient to add that in the past two and a half years, the system which was evolved has yielded astonishing results.

It is impossible to give these results in detail, but certain facts are especially interesting. We have pursued always the policy of consulting our men before effecting radical innovations – the results have been satisfactory to both the men and the company. The men naturally and justifiably grow to feel that the part they play in the company's activities is recognized and, what is even more important, that they are consulted by the management. And that is exactly how we want them to feel. The result is a mutual recognition of interests on the part of the management and the employees which can do no harm and should do a lot of good all around.

THE TWO THINGS ON WHICH THE PULLMAN INNOVATIONS ARE BASED

Our innovations have been based on two separate things; the one, our own system of common-sense management, drawn from our own study of our own peculiar requirements – the other, the Taylor system of scientific management in those certain principles which have been selected from that system as a whole as particularly applicable to our needs.

Tools, for example, formed another source of trouble and expense. In the old days every workman got all the tools he wanted, as many duplicates as he could in addition, and stowed them away in this place or that, where he could "conveniently" get them. The result was that it was impossible to locate anything – thousands of dollars' worth of tools were being constantly lost – the duplicating of tools representing a large investment and the tools were often not in proper condition.

Moreover, every man would himself take his tools to be ground or sharpened – take them at any hour of the day and wait while the work was being done. In the case of a high-priced mechanic this was pretty expensive for the company.

The new system, however, solved this situation. A central tool room was established. Tool boys were employed to go back and forth with the tools, order came out of chaos, thousands of dollars in time and material were saved. Incidentally, it is interesting to state that preparatory to starting the tool room, the buildings were combed for "lost" tools and thousands were recovered.

The handling of the machines was another place of economic weakness. Many of the men didn't know how to use them properly. I remember an instance of our expert watching a man at work with a machine. Somehow it didn't seem to work to his satisfaction and as a result he declared it was "no good." The expert made some quick calculations and suggested that he "speed it up." Reluctantly he complied, and still complained that it was working unsatisfactorily The expert told him to triple the speed. He did so, and immediately the machine performed its work perfectly. The man was willing, but didn't know how – he had no idea that the speed was a factor.

Hand in hand with the development of these lines of effectiveness, constant physical changes are taking place in the plant in order that the men may most efficiently carry out the ideas.

Machines are frequently relocated and grouped, sources of materials are rearranged, even the toilets and rest rooms are moved about so that they are most accessible to the greatest number. A model dispensary has been established, and a hospital for emergency work put in operation.

HERE ARE SOME FACTS ABOUT THE RESULTS WHICH HAVE BEEN SECURED

Of the general results, as far as it is possible accurately to determine, one, of course, is the great saving it has brought to the company.

Today, every man is trying to get the most out of his machine, and the productive efficiency of the individual is being proportionately raised.

The men under this system so fairly enforced, are getting the full value for their labor, and their interest in the system and the unconscious effect of it upon them has been to raise the general tone throughout the entire list of employees.

It is not unreasonable, I think, to hope that the final result will be a condition where labor will be well paid and where men will work in healthful, pleasant and attractive surroundings. This new system of common-sense management which we are using at Pullman is, we hope, a promising path to this desired end.

THE first of the series of articles descriptive of the management policies which the Pullman Company has found so successful, and which President Runnells has just introduced, follows. All of these articles will be edited by Mr. Runnells and transcribed by Mr. Husband under his supervision. This first article, which is short on account of space limitations, will be followed in the March issue by a very detailed article telling how the Pullman Company has applied the principles of the Taylor system of scientific management to its brass foundry. Since for the purposes of this series, at least, this foundry might be an independent enterprise instead of a unit in a large plant known the world over, the March instalment will no doubt be of direct assistance to suitable concerns of every size.

PULLMAN, like many other large manufacturing plants, offers a curiously complete collection of all the various elements that would comprise a complete manufacturing community. In its wide capacity, it buys something of everything; it can make practically anything; it employs almost every kind of artisan and it makes cars – cars in which four thousand separate operations are recorded before the finished sleeper rolls out on the inspection track. Still it has learned lessons from its years of experience which will no doubt benefit and interest the man with a small concern, for some of its detailed activities are comparable with those of average-sized firms.

As with most industrial plants, the early days were marked chiefly by an emphasis on production; unlike the majority, however, the emphasis of recent years has been laid on efficiency of management and manufacture. The results have been startling. Startling not only in the enormous savings all along the line, but in the fact that the production has been increased, higher wages have been paid, better profits have been realized and selling prices have been proportionally reduced.

The story of the repair department at Pullman is perhaps of special interest, because the principles on which its success has been realized are applicable to any manufacturing organization, from the greatest to the very least. There are big and little repair shops by the thousand in this country, and that at Pullman is typical of them, although it does happen to be controlled by a single plant.

There has always been a repair department at Pullman, but formerly it offered little to contrast it with the usual repair department, either independent or subsidiary to the ordinary type of plant. There were machines, tools and repair men; but when something broke down or a tool needed repairing, the workmen tramped whatever distance separated him from the repair shop, lugging the broken article, if possible, and waited idle at so much per hour, while the repairs were made. There were few records, except of the hours of the repair men; no records of machines or idle workmen. It was a comfortable but a costly lack of system.

The repair department of Pullman occupies a comfortably-sized building, practically devoted to its requirements. In it are employed electricians, steamfitters, carpenters, painters, mechanics, riggers, wreckers, and general laborers. About two hundred and fifty men are employed in the department, but perhaps the most interesting member of this staff is the draughtsman.

So varied are the repairs, that routing is naturally impossible, and accordingly it devolves upon the foreman of the section in which the needed repair is located and the draughtsman to determine the procedure. Suppose, for example, a broken shaft on machine 15, shop No. 1, demands attention. A brief minute is all that is necessary to report the accident to the foreman, a few minutes more and the foreman has reported the break to the draughtsman, who starts immediately to make his personal inspection. Meanwhile, if possible, another machine is started and the operator and his job shifted. There is no confusion and practically no loss time.

The draughtsman arriving promptly on the scene, accurately guided by the number of the machine and shop, makes a preliminary inspection to determine if it will be cheaper to make the repair or to purchase out of stock a new part. Presuming, for illustration, that a repair is recommended, he makes a careful sketch and returns to the repair department where the necessary men are sent to remove the broken part, which will be delivered by general laborers to a specified place in the repair department.

The draughtsman now estimates the cost in relation to the age of the machine, and at the same time looks up the record of that particular machine to learn if this accident is a chronic occurrence which might indicate repairs or adjustments to remove the cause of breakdown, or if, perhaps, the workman may be responsible, either because of carelessness or ignorance regarding the proper handling of his machine. The results are carefully noted for further examination.

While these investigations are in progress, a card is made out for the job and hung on the proper hook in the timekeeper's headquarters. Here the repair men receive their instructions in the form of three cards: number one on the upper hook on the board indicates the job in hand; card two, the job waiting at the machine; card three, the job to come. This central point of distribution is the heart of the repair shop. These general principles for the control of the work in the repair shop can, of course, be applied in shops of almost any size.

Guided by the sketches and recommendations of the draughtsman, the repair shop foreman directs what is to be done and the time-card man fills the prescription by determining the workman and machine to perform the work.

Necessarily a fixed hour scale is paid to the repair men, and the foreman and time-keeper become responsible for the distribution of employment.

Resulting from such a system are economies far beyond the not inconsiderable economies of time. First of all, the simplicity of the system has led to an increase in the number of repairs and a consequent decrease in the number of replacements from new stock required. From this increase in repairs comes also a higher degree of upkeep and a consequent improvement in the effectiveness and the quality of manufacture.

ONE RESULT OF A CAREFUL STUDY OF MAINTENANCE COSTS

Like a doctor, the draughtsman has grown to become intimately acquainted with the machines – his patients. He can soon determine the cost of maintenance with an accuracy that has led in repeated instances to the junking of apparently good machines, which in reality were constant consumers of time and materials. With the same facility an accurate check has been effected on the quality of the repair work, for a poor job absolutely identified with the repair man, will soon disclose his carelessness and usually secure better work from him.

Like the five-dollar purse that held the dollar bill, hastily considered repairs are often more expensive than the economy they are planned to make. A review of the records, in one instance, showed that a certain collar cost several dollars, while fifty cents would replace the part that it was intended to protect. The prompt order of the draughtsman to make the collar of another metal which would last, inspection of its wearing effect on the protected part, effected a considerable saving on a large number of machines.

THIS IS A SECTION OF THE PULLMAN COMPANY'S BRASS DEPARTMENT. IT IS IN THE FINISHING SECTION OF THIS DEPARTMENT THAT THE ROUTING SYSTEM DESCRIBED BELOW IS USED

WHAT A NEW SYSTEM OF MANAGEMENT DID FOR US

How the routing methods of the Taylor system of scientific management work

Edited by JOHN S. RUNNELLS — *By* JOSEPH HUSBAND

THIS is the second of the series of articles, entitled "What a New System of Management Did for Us," which John S. Runnells, the president of the Pullman Company, introduced in SYSTEM for February. This series, which will be edited by Mr. Runnells and written under his direction by Joseph Husband, is to tell how a combination of the Taylor system of scientific management with the Pullman Company's own policies and methods effected "astonishing results." This month's instalment and the April instalment describe the routing methods characteristic of the Taylor system. The Pullman Company has applied these methods at heavy expense. This detailed account of exactly how it was done will be of valuable assistance to business men who do not care to assume the heavy expenses, but who realize that the broad principles involved can be taken advantage of by small concerns as well as large ones.

THE development of the system of scientific management at Pullman, a system so aptly called by Mr. Runnells the "common-sense system," reaches its maximum in the brass department. There are, in all, thirty-five general departments in the Pullman plant. Of these, the repair department, which has been considered in a previous article in SYSTEM for February, offers the most interesting development of the non-routing system. But it is in the brass department that routing has reached the perfection of systematization.

The brass department is housed in one of the new buildings, erected in 1910. The building is ideally designed with large window areas, and is of a type of construction adapted to the requirements of brass manufacture. Beyond the heavy steel door that separates the stairway well from the main building, the visitor enters suddenly into the center of the department.

On the right the great workroom, glazed on three sides, rumbles with the voices of the machines. On the columns which support the roof, easily read numbers indicate the various working sections. Around these numbers the machines stand in orderly groups.

Aisles are clear, wide, and straight. There is a noticeable absence of material on the floors. All is order, and efficiency permeates the air. In front of the door, the wire grill of the storeroom discloses rows upon rows of white-painted racks, numbered and complete with the necessary record of their contents.

Even the big bundles of rods and the lengthy strips of metal are neatly stacked in orderly rows. It is impressive. To the left is the office. A door and a window open from it to the main workroom.

If we pass the door, an interesting scene is suddenly presented. The big, bright room is filled with desks, counters, wall racks, and filing devices. Everywhere is activity. Back and forth along the rows of files quick-eyed clerks are passing, moving a card from here to there, marking or initialing, substituting a pink slip for a white one.

There are great loose-leaf ledgers with manila pockets on the backs of the pages. Truly here is all the necessary working machinery for order, precision, accuracy, and efficiency.

But what is it all about? What are these thousand cards, slips, and tickets? What are these racks and files and ledgers? Who are these clerks? What is the purpose?

Had you known the old days, could you know the startling figures of today, you would understand that this is simply the intelligent machinery of bookkeeping for the accurate recording of the costs of a great brass manufactory. Here is a sys-

KIND OF UNIT ______ DESCRIPTION ______ WHEN QUANTITY AVAILABLE FALLS TO ______ SYMBOL S

BALANCE OF STORES ______ ISSUE ORDER FOR ______ LOCATION IN STORES

INSTRUCTIONS FOR POSTING:
A. WHEN STORES ARE ORDERED, ADD THE QUANTITY TO COLUMNS 1 AND 4.
B. WHEN STORES ARRIVE, SUBTRACT THE QUANTITY RECEIVED FROM COLUMN 1 AND ADD THE QUANTITY RECEIVED TO COLUMN 2.
C. WHEN STORES ARE APPORTIONED, SUBTRACT QUANTITY FROM COLUMN 4, AND ADD QUANTITY APPORTIONED TO COLUMN 3.
D. WHEN STORES ARE ISSUED, SUBTRACT QUANTITY FROM COLUMNS 2 AND 3.
NOTE.—IN ALL CASES BRING DOWN AT ONCE BALANCE ON HAND IN EACH COLUMN AFFECTED.

1-STORES ORDERED BUT NOT YET RECEIVED						2-STORES ON HAND IN STOREROOM					3-STORES APPORTIONED TO ORDERS BUT NOT YET ISSUED				4-STORES AVAILABLE THAT IS: ON PURCHASE ORDERS AND ON HAND		
DATE OF REQUISITION	REQUISITION NO.	PURCHASE ORDER NO.	QUANTITY	TOTAL COST	DATE RECEIVED	QUANTITY	DATE ISSUED	ISSUED FOR ORDER NUMBER	TOTAL COST	COST PER UNIT	DATE APPORTIONED	QUANTITY	ORDER NUMBER	DATE ISSUED	DATE	QUANTITY	REMARKS

THE FIRST STEP

This is the record which warned the storekeeper that it was time to order more coathooks. He then made out the stock orders illustrated on pages 284, 285 and 286. From one of these orders the brass department made out the three additional orders described on page 287. These are known as brass department manufacturing orders and differ in color

COPY OF STOCK ORDER

Date Issued 1-19 191 6 ______ Make the following materials and charge S. O. NO. 24449

Deliver to STORE A Stock Distribution A-2

Manifest to STORE A Delivering Dept. PAINT

STOCK ORDER

Date Issued 1-19 191 6 ______ Make the following materials and charge S. O. NO. 24449

Deliver to STORE A Stock Distribution A-2

Manifest to STORE A Delivering Dept. PAINT

Charge to ______ Previous S. O. ______

	Quantity	DESCRIPTION	Finish	Standard No.	Date Allowed for Completion Mo.	Day
	1300	HOOKS, COAT, #174-S, PER DRAWING S-A-10	Ceiling COLOR	5478	8	25
	100	DITTO	MAHG.			
		NO. B/M				

All Departments indicated below by # have been instructed to do work on this order and charge to same all labor and material expended, and handed a copy of this order

Department	Order Comp. Mo.	Day	Department	Order Comp. Mo.	Day	Department	Order Comp. Mo.	Day	Department	Order Comp. Mo.	Day
# Accountant			Pass. Gen. Foreman			Tin			P. L. & M. ( )		
Acct. for P. & S.			Steel Erecting			Upholstery			Lumber		
Chief Engineer			Body Building			Brass Finish (2)			Templet		
			Joining			Pattern			Yard Labor		
Stock Room ___			Trimming			Glass			Drafting		
Shipping Room			Truck and Platform			Electric			Mech. Engineer		
			Cabinet (4)						Watch		
Central Tool			Paint (3)			Freight			Rolling Mill		
Die and Tool			Steam Fitting			Iron (4)			Store Labor		

This space for stamps showing date order completed, etc.

Accounting Dept. record

Total Labor Charges ______ $ ______

Total Material Charges ______ $ ______

Total Labor and Material ______ $ ______

Average Cost Per ______ $ ______

Standard Price Per ______ $ ______

Previous Stock Order No. ______

ORIGINAL

SECOND AND THIRD STEPS

Here is the original order made out by the storekeeper on discovering from his perpetual inventory that his stock of coathooks was running low. There are five duplicates. The first of these duplicates, which is also shown in this illustration, is exactly like the original. It goes immediately to the accounting department. The uses to which the other duplicates are put are indicated by the illustrations on pages 285 and 286

tem so exact and so flexible that its application may be studied for adoption by almost any manufacturer who faces similar problems, a system so adaptable that in the complete or in an abbreviated form it may be applied to a small group of workmen or to a plant many times the size of this department.

Its purpose is economical production combined with that exact knowledge of costs at every operation which is of absolute necessity if the manufacturer of today is to produce at the lowest figure, and by so doing compete successfully with his competitors. Here the system has proved itself.

It can serve others as well. That it has made certain the quality of the product, lightened the labor of the workmen, increased their compensation, and at the same time put money into the treasury of the company, indicates its success.

The easiest way to comprehend the apparent complexity of this system, a system that, understood, is of the most elementary simplicity, is perhaps to follow an order from its start to the final stages when the finished product is delivered to the inspector. The majority of brass articles which enter into car construction demand a more complicated routing, due primarily to the number of operations involved, than it would be possible clearly to follow without previous study of the system. It is, therefore, advisable to select a comparatively simple article, and with this in view I have chosen a brass coathook for the subject of this brief analysis of the system to be given in this article and one to follow it in SYSTEM for April.

In the trimming storeroom the constant inventory (illustrated on page 283) has disclosed the necessity of an additional stock of coathooks, and the storekeeper accordingly estimates his requirements, which, in this instance, are 1,300 coathooks, No. 174-S, "ceiling color," and 100 "mahogany finish." His next step is to put these requirements in written form and start the order through the system. Accordingly, he immediately fills in a stock order with five duplicates, or copies of the stock order, which are illustrated on pages 284, 285 and 286. This order receives an identification number (24449), which will be transcribed on all subsequent orders, move cards, time cards, and the like.

Of this series, the original (see page 284), is retained by the storekeeper in his file. This original not only contains an exact description of the article required, but also a list of thirty-three departments, to any one or more of which the article might pass during the progress of its manufacture.

A cross before such departments indicates instructions to do work on this order and to charge to it such labor and materials as may be used. Furthermore, there is space at the bottom for stamps to indicate the date the order may be completed, as well as an accounting department record, giving total labor charges, total material charges, total labor and material, the average cost, standard price and previous stock-order number. The original stock order will thus become a complete record of manufacture and cost, available for the compilation of data which might at any time be desired.

Having seen the original stock order safely filed in the storekeeper's files, let us turn to the first copy of the stock order (see page 284). This is an exact copy in every detail of the original and is sent immediately to the accounting department.

The second copy (see page 285) differs considerably from the original and the accounting department copy. Here are substituted for the list of the department's and the accountant's records, a record of material ordered, a record of labor, and a record of shipments; and at the bottom of the sheet is a perforated strip receipt, which can be torn off to serve as an acknowledgment.

This copy is delivered to the general foreman of the brass department, who promptly tears off the receipt and mails it to the general storekeeper's offices. The order is now forwarded to the order desk, where we will later meet it after we have observed the departures of the remaining copies.

COPY OF STOCK ORDER

Date Issued 1-19 191 6 ______ Make the following materials and charge S. O. NO. 24449

Deliver to STORE A — Stock Distribution A-2

Manifest No. STORE A — Delivering Dept. PAINT

Charge to ______ — Previous S. O. ______

	Quantity	DESCRIPTION	Finish	Standard No.	Date Allowed for Completion Mo.	Day
	1300	HOOKS, COAT, #174-S, PER DRAWING 3-A-10	CEILING COLOR	5478	8	25
	100	DITTO	MAHO.			
		NO. B/M				

RECORD OF MATERIAL ORDERED

Req. No.	Req. No.	Req. No.	Req. No.	Req. No.	Req. No.

RECORD OF LABOR

Check or Contract No.	Date or Price	Hours or Amount	Check or Contract No.	Date or Price	Hours or Amount	Check or Contract No.	Date or Price	Hours or Amount

RECORD OF SHIPMENTS

Date Mo.	Day	Manifest No.	Quantity	Date Mo.	Day	Manifest No.	Quantity	Date Mo.	Day	Manifest No.	Quantity

I hereby acknowledge receipt of ______ copies of S. O. No. 24449

BR. FIN. Dept. ______ Foreman

Mail this receipt promptly to General Storekeeper's Office

FOURTH STEP

This is the second duplicate of the original stock order shown on page 284. This copy is delivered to the general foreman of the brass department, who promptly tears off the receipt and mails it to the general storekeeper's offices. Then it goes to the brass department order desk. The brass department order clerk then begins the second stage of the routing by writing out the manufacturing orders. These orders are discussed on page 287

COPY OF STOCK ORDER

Date Issued 1-19 191 6 ______ Make the following materials and charge S. O. NO. 24449

Deliver to STORE A — Stock Distribution A-2

Manifest to STORE A — Delivering Dept. PAINT

Charge to ______ — Previous S. O. ______

	Quantity	DESCRIPTION	Finish	Standard No.	Date Allowed for Completion	
					Mo.	Day
	1300	HOOKS, COAT, #174-S, PER DRAWING 3-A-10.	CEILING COLOR	5478	8	25
	100	DITTO.	MAHG.			
		No. B/M.				

RECORD OF MATERIAL ORDERED

Requisition No.	Requisition No.	Requisition No.	Requisition No.	Requisition No.	Requisition No.

FIFTH STEP

This is the third duplicate of the stock order shown on page 284. It contains only a record of material ordered. This copy, like the second, is sent to the brass department order desk

SIXTH STEP

This is the fourth duplicate of the stock order shown on page 284. It goes to the accountant for the purchase of stores

COPY OF STOCK ORDER

Date Issued 1-19 191 6 ______ Make the following materials and charge S. O. NO. 24449

Deliver to STORE A — Stock Distribution A-2

Manifest to STORE A — Delivering Dept. PAINT

Charge to ______ — Previous S. O. ______

	Quantity	DESCRIPTION	Finish	Standard No.	Date Allowed for Completion	
					Mo.	Day
	1300	HOOKS, COAT, #174-S, PER DRAWING 3-A-10	CEILING COLOR	5478	8	25
	100	DITTO	MAHG.			
		NO. B/M				

COPY FOR ACCOUNTANT FOR PURCHASES AND STORES

STORE DEPARTMENT COPY OF STOCK ORDER

Date Issued 1-19 191 6 ______ Make the following materials and charge S. O. NO. 24449

Deliver to STORE A — Stock Distribution A-2

Manifest to STORE A — Delivering Dept. PAINT

Charge to ______ — Previous S. O. ______

	Quantity	DESCRIPTION	Finish	Standard No.	Date Allowed for Completion	
					Mo.	Day
	1300	HOOKS, COAT, #174-S, PER DRAWING 3-4-10	CEILING COLOR	5478	8	25
	100	DITTO	MAHO			
		NO. B/M				

RECORD OF RECEIPTS

Date		Manifest No.	Quantity	Date		Manifest No.	Quantity	Date		Manifest No.	Quantity	Date		Manifest No.	Quantity
Mo.	Day			Mo.	Day			Mo.	Day			Mo.	Day		

STOCKROOM ______ COPY

LAST STEP

This is the fifth duplicate of the stock order shown on page 284. It goes to the individual stockroom requiring the material, where it will serve as a complete record of receipts as the order is delivered

The next copy (see page 286), besides the necessary description of the order, contains only a record of material ordered. This copy, like the second, is sent to the brass department order desk.

Copy number four (see page 286) goes to the accountant for the purchase of stores, and the last copy (see page 286) goes to the individual stockroom requiring the material, where it will serve as a record of receipts as the order is delivered. For this purpose it contains a form for the recording of the date, manifest number, and quantity.

THIS IS HOW THE SECOND STAGE IN THE ROUTING BEGINS

It is now apparent that of these five sheets, the second copy (see page 285) is the active member from which further orders are filled out. We had left this stock order at the order desk, to which it had been sent by the department general foreman. Here the order clerk begins the second stage of the routing by writing out orders in triplicate (in three colors, also), which are known as brass department manufacturing orders, which for convenience we will designate as A (yellow), B (pink) and C (white).

These three brass department orders differ in color, being printed on yellow, pink and white paper, respectively. All are identical, giving in the upper right-hand corner the month, day and year in which the order was issued, the date on which the order is required, and spaces for the date on which the order will be finished. The orders further describe the article, and the number required, and contain spaces for tickler checking dates.

The most interesting feature of these orders, however, is the series of stages of progress which are indicated along the bottom. Here the day and hour are filled in as each step is taken, and the initials of the clerk are recorded. Thus the first compartment is entitled "order written"; the second, "drawings and bills of material prepared"; the third, "stores issue written, materials apportioned and requisition written, foundry tags written, routing laid out, rates set, route file prepared, cost card written, materials delivered to shop, work started, work finished, and cost prepared." As these steps are recorded by the dates and initials, a heavy pencil line is drawn from the left to the right, graphically showing at a glance the exact point which has been reached.

It has been noted in the preceding paragraph that the brass department manufacturing order is written in triplicate on differently colored forms. We will, for the time being, dispose of two of these forms which are comparatively inactive.

Of these, the yellow form (A) is known as the "record copy" and goes on file at the manufacturing order clerk's desk file, and there is marked as such successive operations as are required are performed. It is necessary at this point also to explain about the filing system at the order desk. It consists of a file with fourteen double pockets corresponding to the fourteen compartments across the bottom of the order. This file is a permanent wooden case. Between the upper and lower lines of double pockets, which are in a row seven pockets long and two high, is a permanent black line which subdivides the top row from the bottom in order to assist in the avoidance of errors in filing. In the top pockets are placed the pink and white orders indicating "work to be done," a movement to the lower pockets indicating "work in progress."

The yellow order on the permanent record file indicates at any time the progress of the work by the long pencil line and the filling in of the lower compartments.

We have now filed the yellow order (A); and the copy of the stock orders, having performed its function, is also filed away. The pink order (B), being the tickler copy, remains at the order desk case in that one of the fourteen pockets which represents the desk at which the white order, which is the circulating copy, (C), happens to be. When all the work in the office is completed, the pink order (B) is retained as a tickler copy.

THIS ORDER IS CUMULATIVE AND ADDS TO ITSELF OTHER TAGS AND FORMS

The white brass department manufacturing order (C) has been mentioned as the circulating copy. It is this order which passes through the office, going to the various desks for drawings and bills of materials, stores issue and the like, to be written in and filled.

At the first desk the bill of material clerk fills in the date, and initials the second compartment. He also prepares the required bill of material in duplicate. This bill of material is described below. The duplicate bill is now filed for the record of the receipt of the material, and the original accompanies the white circulating brass department manufacturing order (C) to the requisition desk for stores issue tags to be written. It is thus seen that the circulating brass department manufacturing order is cumulative, adding other forms and tags to itself as it progresses among the various required desks.

The bill of material, or statement of stores issue, is a large form containing double spaces for eighteen items, department numbers, stockroom identification letters, requisition numbers and quantity of items required. There are other spaces for description, standard or pattern number, quantity delivered, price, amount, and the stock distribution. The reverse contains rulings for the stock distribution.

At this point it must be explained that should a new article be called for, which has never before been manufactured, the original order emanates from the engineer's office, which forwards the drawing, the bill of material, and the necessary information regarding sizes, shapes, design and finish.

The statement of stores issue, attached to the white brass department manufacturing order (C), now serves as an information source from which the stores issue clerk makes out his stores issue, which is an order on the storekeeper for the stores required. At the same time, he prepares a statement called the "worked materials received in stores."

When material is delivered on a stores issue form, delivery is marked and forwarded to the accountant. The stores issue order contains the location for delivery, the quantity, the kind of unit, the cost per unit and the total value, together with the necessary symbols for charging and spaces for dating and receipting. The issuance of the order is now checked on the "stores issue written" compartment of the white circulating brass department order (C).

The circulating order now progresses, with stores issue order and its duplicate, which has been apportioned by the balance clerk on the stock record; and a tag for tagging material, when delivered from the storerooms, is added. This storeroom is a sub-storeroom located in the building. Also two tags and the tag for worked material for assembling are added, together with a fourth tag for stores for worked materials.

It is the further duty of the "materials apportioned and requisition written" desk to fill out forms – worked materials issued – to be signed by the storekeeper, and a duplicate – worked materials credited – and another duplicate, also to be signed by the storekeeper, and a stores credited slip and its duplicate, also for the storekeeper's signature.

The white circulating brass department manufacturing order (C) now progresses to the route clerk, who prepares the route sheet, fills in the column heading and signs it.

Of this route sheet I will write, under Mr. Runnells's direction, in SYSTEM for April. This will complete my description of the preliminary detail of the writing of the orders, tags and cards, and place us in readiness to observe them in actual operation.

FROM such a storeroom as this the orders for stock referred to in the accompanying article are filled. The racks are numbered to make rapid reference to their contents possible and the double compartments containing small articles are removable so as to facilitate replenishment. Emptying one side of a double compartment automatically signals the need of replenishment. The cards slipped into the racks on the compartments supply data on the contents, stock limits and the like

WHAT A NEW SYSTEM OF MANAGEMENT DID FOR US

This article tells how another part of the Pullman plant is managed. Here a detailed system of scientific management has been installed by an expert of wide experience

Edited by JOHN S. RUNNELLS | *By* JOSEPH HUSBAND

WHEN "common-sense management," President Runnells's phrase for describing the Pullman adoption of scientific management, was first instituted in the great shops at Pullman, there were certain departments where the new practices found readier application than in others. As a whole, the system was radical and fairly sweeping in its application. During long years of growth wasteful ways had been fostered, losses, inaccuracies and confusing unrelated systems had been spontaneously developed. To this great organization, as to many smaller manufacturers throughout the country during recent years, had come the realization that conditions were bad and methods slipshod. And like all concerns who have watched the amazing discoveries of modern business, the Pullman executives recognized the strides that had been made in business science, and as quickly as possible sought to profit by the application of these tested principles, adjusted by good common sense to their own problems.

The interest of the Pullman story to business men today is the fact that the size and diversity of manufacture of the Pullman Company has enabled it to apply manufacturing science to a wide variety of highly specialized departments, correlate these into a coherent scheme and soundly test the efficacy of the system which today characterizes a progressive manufacturer.

The brass department is a peculiarly noticeable example of the application of pure scientific management. Including its own pattern shop and foundry, it contains within itself all the elements of a manufacturing plant that might, for all appearances, be absolutely distinct from the great organization of which it is a unit.

What has been done in the Pullman brass department may be as successfully accomplished in Peoria or Bridgeport. The system was adopted in order to make money by reducing costs. The system has done it. This is of interest to every manufacturer. Of equal interest is the description of how the system was applied. In the March issue of SYSTEM the elaborate scheme of routing was partially described and the description will be concluded in this number. But before taking up the continuation of the routing system, certain points may need a little emphasis.

In former days approximately seven men conducted the operation of the brass department and its three hundred and fifty workmen. Today, under scientific management, forty-seven men are required to direct the work of the same number of workmen. Here is a vast increase in overhead, for one thousand dollars a year for each of the forty-seven is a fair average for the type of man required successfully to apply so elaborate a system. But does it pay? It has certainly done so! The actual saving of about one hundred dollars a car in this one department has wiped out additional overhead and showed substantial profits. What is the reason?

THE RESULTS OF CONCENTRATING THE WORK OF THE DEPARTMENT IN ONE PLACE

Out of the Pullman brass department comes the great truth of scientific management. Where once but seven men apparently contributed their efforts, in many places throughout the plant one man or another was devoting a part of his time to assist the active seven. All the planning was being done somewhere. And every man contributing by that much demoralized his own particular work by the interruption. Now all is done in one place by men who do nothing else – and no one else can be distracted by the problems of the brass department or disturb its operation by unrequired interference.

With the elimination of unseen elements of contributing management were eliminated also the hours wasted by workmen from other departments who were accustomed to come with this or that job and "wait" until the work was completed. One of the first steps was to cut off the brass department; doors were locked and windows screened. If anything came in, it must come through regular channels.

With the increased efficiency of the workmen came an increased improvement of manufacture that is hard to estimate, but should be considered of

ROUTE SHEET

PIECE SYMBOL M 5 4 2 0 N

DESCRIPTION OF PIECE: #1745 Coat or Razor Strop Hook DRAWING No. 3-A-10

REMARKS: Mall Iron PATTERN No. T5395

WEIGHT EACH

DATE ORDERED	4-19-15	7-21-15	9-7-15	9-21-15	11-11-15	1-7-16
DATE WANTED	6-21-15	8-25-15	10-1-15	10-28-15	1-15-16	2-15-16
LOT No.	7	8	9	10	11	12
CHARGE TO	M.O. 22799	24449	25630	25944	27778	29110-1
ORIGINAL NUMBER PIECES IN LOT	1450	1400	800	1400	3000	1065

DESCRIPTION OF OPERATION	ALTERNATIVE MACHINE	STANDARD MACHINE	LOCATION	OPERATION NUMBER	PIECES O. K. AFTER FINAL INSPECTION (RCE)	PIECES O. K. AFTER FINAL INSPECTION (RCE)	PIECES O. K. AFTER FINAL INSPECTION (RCE)	PIECES O. K. AFTER FINAL INSPECTION (RCE)	PIECES O. K. AFTER FINAL INSPECTION (RCE)	PIECES O. K. AFTER FINAL INSPECTION (RCE)
FROM STOREROOM B — MATERIAL ORDERED										
1. Polish — MATERIAL IN STORES		GP	D2B	1	8GE1	1000 8GE	1GP1	2GP3	3GP1	
2. Jig drill 2 holes		8DV	D2B	2	1000 8DV8	8DV5	8DV5	8DV5	8DV5	
.0005 3. Countersink (#6)		8DV	D2B	3		8DV5	8DV5	8DV5	8DV5	
4. Sandblast		XS	D1B	4						
5. Inspect			D1B3C	5						
6. Paint		Paint	D2B	6						
MOVE TO STOREROOM A										
					5-11-15	8-4-15	10-16-15	10-13-15		

THE ROUTE SHEET

The route sheet measures about twenty by fourteen inches and is kept in loose-leaf form for binding in a large folder. Facing each route sheet in the route file book, or filing book, is a manila sheet containing six pockets in which are kept the cards required to carry out the various operations

high importance. The old lack of method never is and never will be conducive to a betterment of standards, but systemization promptly showed a surprising rise in quality; workmen concentrated and the product showed the result.

Another interesting aspect is aptly described by Eugene Morris, who has been largely responsible for the successful development of The Pullman system. "Our system of common-sense management brings trouble quickly to the surface." There it is. All may seem clear and placid. Your factory produces its required output with its normal increase of volume at its accepted cost. Touch it with the acid of systematic management; losses, inaccuracies, conditions almost unbelievable, will float to the surface.

In the last number my description of the Pullman routing system closed with a description of the preliminary detail of the writing of some of the more important orders, tags and cards involved in its operation. This brought me to the route sheet, which I will now discuss.

The route sheet measures about twenty by fourteen inches and is kept in loose-leaf form for binding in a large folder. It contains a description of operations, move routing, spaces for "material ordered," and "material in stores," which are marked off with a blue stamp when checked; a listing of specified machines with their location and the operation number, and columns for an inspection checking of the various operations. Blue stamps at the top and bottom of these columns and vertical pencil lines graphically illustrate the progress of the work.

Facing each route sheet in the route file board, or filing book, is a manila sheet containing six pockets. Wherever the book is opened the route sheet, accordingly, is the right-hand page, the manila on the left. In these pockets are kept the cards required to carry out the operations. Here they remain until the material is available at the machines, when they are removed and placed in the machine boxes in the planning department. These boxes will be described in SYSTEM for May.

The white circulating brass department manufacturing order now moves on to the route file prepared desk, where it is the time card clerk's duty to prepare the necessary move cards, time cards and carry-over cards.

Time cards are made in triplicate from the route sheet. The pink original gives spaces for the workman's name and number; the operation number; piece symbol; lot number; description of operation; alternative and standard machines, and their locations; descriptions of articles, and other information. At the bottom are five squares entitled respectively "material, "data," "means," "started," "finished." These are filled in with a pencil line by the department clerk at the shop foreman's board.

As I have already stated, this is a pink ticket. The duplicate is blue, and in place of the spaces for recording the progress of the work, contains spaces to indicate the number of pieces previously condemned by the inspector; the number of pieces condemned at a given operation; the number of pieces finished at a given operation, together with spaces for the inspector's initials and spaces directing the movement of the article, with the second location indicated, and spaces for the initials of the men by whom moved and by whom received. The triplicate is a white card. This is really the time card and contains spaces for data showing the number of pieces finished on a given day; the machine time, the cost number and relative cost; the man's time; man's

BRASS DEPARTMENT ORDER S. O 24449

PLEASE MACHINE / ASSEMBLE THE FOLLOWING:

ORDER ISSUED			ORDER WANTED			ORDER FINISHED		
MONTH	DAY	YEAR	MONTH	DAY	YEAR	MONTH	DAY	YEAR
1	19	1916	3	19	1916			19

NUMBER OF PIECES IN LOT	SYMBOL OF ARTICLE	PATTERN NO.	DRAWING NO.	DESCRIPTION OF ARTICLE
1400	M 5420 N			174 ½ Razor Strop Hooks

REMARKS: Mahogany Finish

SIGNED Glen S. Harrison

ORDER WRITTEN		DRAWINGS AND BILLS OF M'T'L PREPARED		STORES ISSUES WRITTEN		MATERIALS APPORT'D AND REQ. WRITTEN		FOUNDRY TAGS WRITTEN		ROUTING LAID OUT		RATES SET		ROUTE FILE PREPARED		REQ. OR STORES ISSUES CLEARED		COST CARD WRITTEN		MATERIALS DELIVERED TO SHOP		WORK STARTED		WORK FINISHED		COST PREPARED	
DAY	HOUR	DAY	HOUR	DAY	HOUR	DAY	HOUR	DAY	HOUR	DAY	HOUR	DAY	HOUR	DAY	HOUR	DAY	HOUR	DAY	HOUR	DAY	HOUR	DAY	HOUR	DAY	HOUR	DAY	HOUR
1/19	11 30 a	19	11/40	1/19	11/50	19	12 00	X	X	1/19	1/30			1/19	1/40	1/19	1/50	X	X	1	19	X	X	1	19		
H		DOC		MS		W		X		RCJ				MB		MD		X		B		X		B			

THE MANUFACTURING ORDERS

One of the orders is pink, another white, and the third yellow. The pink order is dated and filed in the tickler. The white, or circulating order, is first filed "awaiting delivery." The yellow order, after being temporarily filed, is sent to the requisition clerk's "live" file

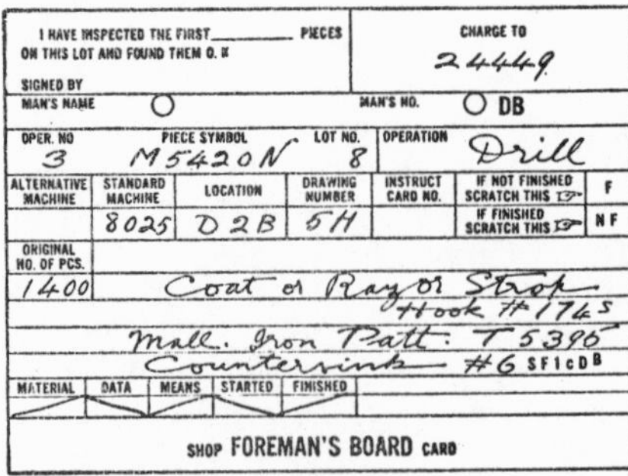

I HAVE INSPECTED THE FIRST ______ PIECES ON THIS LOT AND FOUND THEM O. K
SIGNED BY
CHARGE TO 24449
MAN'S NAME | MAN'S NO. DB
OPER. NO 3 | PIECE SYMBOL M5420N | LOT NO. 8 | OPERATION Drill
ALTERNATIVE MACHINE | STANDARD MACHINE 8025 | LOCATION D2B | DRAWING NUMBER 5H | INSTRUCT CARD NO. | IF NOT FINISHED SCRATCH THIS F | IF FINISHED SCRATCH THIS NF
ORIGINAL NO. OF PCS. 1400
Coat or Razor Strop Hook #1745
Mall. Iron Patt. T5395
Countersink #6 SF1cD B
MATERIAL | DATA | MEANS | STARTED | FINISHED
SHOP FOREMAN'S BOARD CARD

THE ORIGINAL TIME CARD (PINK)

This card, which marks the first operation, is sent to the shop foreman's board when the required material is ready. The foreman traces the progress of the work on it in the lower left-hand space. As soon as the work is under way it becomes an inspection ticket

REC'D
ISSUED
CHARGE TO 24449
MAN'S NAME | MAN'S NO.
OPER. NO. 3 | PIECE SYMBOL M5420N | LOT NO. 8 | OPERATION Drill
ALTERNATIVE MACHINE | STANDARD MACHINE 8025 | LOCATION D2B | DRAWING NUMBER 5H | INSTRUCT CARD NO. | IF NOT FINISHED SCRATCH THIS F | IF FINISHED SCRATCH THIS NF
ORIGINAL NO. OF PCS. 1400
Coat or Razor Strop Hook #1745
Mall. Iron Patt. T5395
Countersink #6 SF1bD B
NO. OF PIECES PREVIOUSLY CONDEMNED | NO. OF PIECES CONDEMNED THIS OPERATION | NO. OF PIECES FINISHED THIS OPERATION | INSPECTED BY SIGNED
MOVE TO | MOVED BY SIGNED
ROUTE SHEET | INSPECTION AND MOVE CARD | LOCATION | RECEIVED BY SIGNED

THE DUPLICATE COPY (BLUE)

The time cards are made out in triplicate from the route sheet. This blue duplicate is used for the final inspection and provides suitable spaces for recording data about previous output, the inspector's initials, and directions regarding the movement of the work

REC'D 916 JAN 19 PM 4 10
ISSUED 916 JAN 19 PM 4 10
CHARGE TO 24449
MAN'S NAME W. Small | MAN'S NO. 8540
OPER. NO 3 | PIECE SYMBOL M5420N | LOT NO. 8 | OPERATION Drill
ALTERNATIVE MACHINE | STANDARD MACHINE 8025 | LOCATION D2B | DRAWING NUMBER 5H | INSTRUCT CARD NO. | IF NOT FINISHED SCRATCH THIS F | IF FINISHED SCRATCH THIS NF
ORIGINAL NO. OF PCS. 1400
Coat or Razor Strop Hook #1745
Mall. Iron Patt. T5395
Countersink #6 SF1aD B
NO. OF PIECES FINISHED TODAY 1400 | 1400 MACHINE due | TIME | COST NO. | REL. COST | MAN'S TIME | MAN'S RATE | RATE .06 PER C | PIECE RATE EARNINGS
ROUTE SHEET | PAY ROLL | MAN'S COST | MACH. COST | MAN'S JOB CARD P. W. | DAY WORK EARNINGS

THE TRIPLICATE COPY (WHITE)

This white triplicate is really the time card and contains spaces for data showing the number of pieces finished on a given day; the machine time, the cost, number and relative cost; the workman's time; workman's rate; workman's charge; machine charge; piece earnings; and day earnings

rate; man's cost; machine's cost; piece rate earnings; and day work earnings.

The move card is made out at the same time from the route sheet, and is sent with the white circulating brass department manufacturing order to the requisition and stores issues cleared clerk, who forwards the stores issues card, together with the move card, to the storeroom. At the same time the piecework carry-over card is made out, attached to time cards, and all are filed.

We have now completed the preliminary detail of the writing of the orders, tags, and cards, and are ready to observe them in actual operation.

It has been noted that the pink brass department manufacturing order has been dated and filed in the tickler. The white circulating order is filed "waiting delivery." And the yellow order is still on file with all the office work completed. The production clerk now is advised by his tickler order to take out the stores issues cards, move cards, and tags from the files, and send them to the clearing clerk who files them in a "live" file. He also removes from the files the yellow order and also forwards it to the requisition clerk for his "live" file. He now gives the move card, stores issues card and tag to the move man who takes them to the storeroom for material and proceeds with the tagged material to the shop foreman designated, who in time signs for the material and directs it to the first operation work place. These receipted stores issues now return to the storeroom storekeeper, who notes them and sends them to the balance clerk, who enters them. They are next sent back to the clearing clerk, who checks them against his other duplicates and sends the originals to the accountant for the compilation of costs.

The move card is signed by the recording clerk of the route file, who marks it with the jobs. Banked against the walls in one corner of the office are the machine boxes. Here are a series of three pockets in three steps. Into a set of

MOVE CARD PLEASE MOVE THIS MATERIAL TO MACHINE FOR NEXT UNSIGNED OPERATION			PIECE SYMBOL M 5420 N			LOT NO. 121
NO. OF PCS. 1065	3-A-10 T 5395		CHARGE TO 29110 —1			
DESCRIPTION #174S Coat or Razor Strop Hook						
OPER. NO.	STANDARD MACHINE	LOCATION	ALTERNATIVE MACHINE	SIGNED MOVEMAN	SIGNED FOREMAN	ENTERED ON ROUTE SHEET
	STORES					
1	G P	D 2 B				
2	80 L	"				
3	80 L	"				
4	XS	D 1 B				
5	Inspect					
6	Paint	D 2 B				
7	Store A					
8						
9						
0						

THE MOVE CARD

The move card is made out at the same time from the route sheet, and is sent together with the white circulating brass department manufacturing order and the stores issues card to the storeroom

PIECE WORK CARRY OVER CARD					CHARGE BONUS ONLY TO 3- M5420 N-8	
ORIG. NO. PCS. IN LOT	MAN'S NAME			MAN'S NO. DB		
1400	RECORD OF TIME WORKED AND AMOUNT ADVANCED ON PIECE WORK JOB 24449					
NO. PIECES FINISHED	MONTH	DAY	DAY OF WEEK	TIME WORKED HOURS TENTHS	MACHINE NUMBER	
					*C = RATE PER PIECE	.05
			Ctsk		B = NO. OF GOOD PIECES FINISHED	
					C = A X B = TOTAL AMOUNT EARNED ON JOB	70
					D = TOTAL TIME WORKED	
	TOTAL NO. OF PCS. FINISHED		TOTAL TIME WORKED		E = D X MAN'S ADVANCE RATE — AM'T ALREADY PAID	
TIME CLERK	PAY ROLL	COST SHEET		BONUS = C — E =		

THE PIECEWORK CARRY-OVER CARD

The piecework carry-over card is made out at the same time that the move cards and stores issues cards are filled in. It is attached to the time cards, and when the work is finished all are filed together

these pockets the order of work clerk assigns the particular job in question and sorts the triplicate time cards. This marks the actual starting of the work. First, the pink ticket marking the first operation is sent to the shop foreman's board, in the instance only that material is available. If the material, however, is not available all three copies go into the third or last pocket of the machine box. Presuming that material is available, the blue and white tickets are placed in the second pocket, indicating the machines to which the order of work clerk has assigned the job. This for the first operation on the article to be manufactured, only. All other tickets are put in the upper or third pocket ready at hand for use when needed.

As soon as the move ticket returns to the office, indicating that the material has been delivered, the pink ticket is sent to the foreman's board where it is placed following the previous jobs in the order that they are required by the shop. The foreman's board in the brass department contains five positions: one for work in progress, three for material awaiting operations at the machine, and one for cards for additional work assigned to the machine, for which material is available, but not necessarily at the machine. The foreman now investigates regarding material, and if all is delivered draws a pencil line through the first space in the lower left-hand corner of the pocket. If blue prints and other necessary information are at hand he marks the space "Data" with a similar line. If tools are ready he marks likewise the space "Means." The space "Started" is marked when the job starts; "Finished" when it is completed.

As soon as the job is under way the pink ticket becomes an inspection ticket, to be filled in by the inspector, and is returned to the file when the job is completed. The blue ticket is used for final inspection. The workman on completing the job comes immediately to the planning department for the next job. The cards are now advanced in the machine boxes and on the foreman's board, the workman receiving the original, the blue copy being retained in the first position to show the material being worked at each machine.

A machine box is assigned to every machine and work place in the department. This box bears the symbol of the machine and a brass identification check. In addition, there is a "Man's Board," assigning a check to every man in the department, and a brass check bearing his number. These boards form a cross index. The workman's brass check – which is different in shape from the machine brass check – is hung on the machine box hook to which he has been assigned; the machine check is placed on a peg on the "Man's Board" opposite the man assigned to the machine.

Upon the final return of the time cards to the planning department, the route sheets are posted and an exact and graphic record of the condition of the job is instantly available.

A natural impression from the study of this article in minds unfamiliar with a complete system of routing may be that the progress of work might be hampered by the transaction of the required detail. But this is far from the case. Such a system demands primarily a clearly conceived plan devised to meet actual conditions and current needs. Secondly, it requires a competent staff in the office department to transact the detail. Here is the great volume of the work – practically all is accomplished by trained clerks and the workman is left undisturbed to devote his entire energy to the accomplishment of his job. To the workman are delegated no complicated time cards to estimate; he has no interest in the sources of his material or the place to which the article on which he labors will move. Everything is supplied to him, quickly, automatically. His product is removed as he completes it. No matter how fast he may hurry, the flow of new material comes uninterruptedly and without crowding; unfailingly the move men pass on his product.

Such a system is not practical in its entirety for every plant or for any department. At Pullman it is only in the brass department that this complete system of routing has been installed. To be sure, it is to be adapted to other departments, but there are some, such as the repair department, for which it could never give the desired service.

For the average manufacturer, however, there is much of value in a study of this system. The Pullman Company has profited by its adoption; the workmen have profited; a better product has resulted. Under careful study, the system resolves itself into an extremely simple proposition, easily adapted to a wide range of requirements.

HOW SPECIAL TOOLS ARE ISSUED

A three months' supply of tools, valued at $90,000, is carried in the central tool room. The run of tools are issued from branches in the various departments. These men are applying directly to the central tool room for special tools which must be returned before closing time

WHAT A NEW SYSTEM OF MANAGEMENT DID FOR US

This plan is not complicated, it can be used in either large or small concerns, it is not new – and in one department alone it saved the Pullman Company $39,000

Edited by JOHN S. RUNNELLS

By JOSEPH HUSBAND

THIS series of articles has to do with an unusual industrial situation. The Pullman Company has at great expense developed what its officials call a "common-sense system of management." Many of these lessons, which the Pullman Company has learned at an expense which but few concerns could undertake, are of value to small concerns as well as large ones, for the Pullman Company's plant is in fact but an assemblage of small productive units into one great organization.

The development of this system of management is of unusual interest because in developing it the Pullman Company has made use of several systems of scientific management. In one part of the plant one of these was installed practically entire; in another the Pullman Company's variations of it; in still others, only the Company's ideas of management ideas. Hence an all but unique picture of modern practice in development is available.

It is the purpose of these articles to trace this development. The first of them – published in SYSTEM for February – described a Pullman repair shop which uses an adaptation of a standard routing system. The March and April instalments referred to the Pullman brass department, which uses a standard system in its entirety. And this article describes the central tool-room system, which merges into a happy combination many standardized ideas and many ideas originated within the Pullman organization by Mr. Runnells and his assistants.

The central tool room at Pullman is not, of course, an innovation in shop practice; it is in use in countless American factories. That, however, is worth study not only because it typifies this interesting combination of ideas, but marks a step in business practice that is important to business men in every line and which must be taken by many businesses, both large and small. It marks a stepping away from tradition in order to search about free of mind and hand for the one best way.

Tools had usually been kept in the old way. The Pullman officials took a fresh viewpoint, determined to find the right way, the common-sense way, no matter what had been done for years. And a new and a more economical way of keeping tools resulted.

It is by taking a fresh stand in much the same way that leads a now successful grocer to sell for cash only where credits have formerly been used; that leads a now successful wholesaler to distribute in a more economical way after abandoning methods that had become traditional in his line. So in addition to being a description of a method of handling tools that should be of value to large and small businesses using tools, this article reflects a great fundamental business step of interest in every line of commercial activity.

Like the heart in a human body the central tool room of the Pullman plant performs a constant and a vital function that reaches ultimately to every one of the six thousand workmen and to the farthest corners of the great plant that embraces two square miles of prairie.

In the earlier days, before the inception of modern methods of common-sense management, there was no central tool room, and the circulation was weak and wasteful. There are eighteen departments in the Pullman plant, departments as different in their functions as those of separate industries in a manufacturing community, but all tied firmly in a perfect working system that produces cars, – cars that we call "Pullmans," freight cars, street cars, subway cars, nothing but cars, and all of steel.

Formerly each department had its individual tool room. Under this method, the natural development of a great plant along lines not characterized by a sense of systemization, it was customary for the

TOOL CARD NO. 172

NAME H. F. Wamelink

DEPARTMENT Machining CHECK NO. 25

AIR HAMMERS	
" DRILLS	
ELECTRIC DRILLS	2
DRILLS	
"	
"	
REAMERS	
"	
"	
TAPS	
FILES	3 round – 12"
SOCKETS	

DATE	THE ABOVE TOOLS TO BE SURRENDERED IN CASE OF EMPLOYEE BEING TRANSFERRED OR LEAVING SERVICE
3/25/16	C. Borewell
	EMPLOYEE WILL BE HELD STRICTLY ACCOUNTABLE FOR ABOVE TOOLS

The EMPLOYEE'S TOOL CARD

When he is employed each workman receives from his foreman an order like this for his initial tool equipment, which he presents to the sub-tool room in his department and gets his tools

DATE 3/29/16 — STATEMENT OF BROKEN TOOLS FROM CAGE NO. 7 — CHARGE TO DEPT. B.O.2

DRILLS			REAMERS			TAPS			MISCELLANEOUS	
CHECK NO.	QUANTITY	SIZE	CHECK NO.	QUANTITY	SIZE	CHECK NO.	QUANTITY	SIZE	CHECK NO.	DESCRIPTION
1028	1	3/16	1028	1	57/64	1028	3	1/2"	865	1-3/4 Pipe Die
1538	1	11/16	2065	2	3/4				1005	1-14" F.B. File
865	2	1/2							1227	1-Ele Socket
1005	3	3/4								
1128	1	1/2								

TOOL CAGE KEEPER

The LIST OF BROKEN TOOLS

Stuck in each of the tote boxes in which broken or worn tools are collected is a form like this. The tools collected are listed on it by the man who fills the box. The workmen's numbers are recorded so that the care with which each man handles his tools may be learned

CAGE NO. — NO. 6

CHECK NO. — DATE

QUANTITY	SIZE	KIND OF TOOL	UNIT PRICE	AMOUNT
3	9/64	Drills Carbon S.S.	2 3/10	6 9/10
1	#14/20	Taps	3 9/10	3 9/10
2	14"	Flat Bastard File	18 1/2	37 1/2

BAL. SHEET	EXTEND	CHECKED	STOCK CLASSIFICATION	TOTAL
A	E	W	TOOLS – CENTRAL TOOL	48 7/15

SIGNED Fred Brown

FOR ADDITIONAL TOOLS

When tools are broken or dulled, substitutes are supplied on requisitions like this. The workmen sign these requisitions as they receive the fresh tools. Twice a year a special check is made against a perpetual inventory and the records resulting from these requisitions

men to draw the tools they required by the simple method of a personal call at their tool room. Few questions were asked and, as it was easier to get a new tool than to find a mislaid one, the duplication in a short time reached amazing proportions.

Also it was necessary for the men to keep their own tools in repair. Such practice resulted in a decreased efficiency of the tools in use, for a good workman is not necessarily an experienced repair man, nor is he always qualified to grind a dulled edge to the highest cutting efficiency.

Another circumstance should be considered as having considerable bearing on the necessity of a system of centralized tool control. Up to the time when the system described in this article was inaugurated the greater proportion of all Pullman cars were constructed of wood. As it is customary for carpenters to provide and care for their own tools, the necessity of a new system became acute with the rapid increase of steel-car manufacture. In this work tools must be provided, and, in addition, the wear on the tools was immeasurably increased. Today only steel cars are manufactured by the Pullman Company.

With the development of the new system came the centralization of the tool rooms. One by one the various tool rooms were cleaned up and stock was taken. That one department alone showed a stock of surplus tools to the value of $39,000 indicates the point that had been reached. As soon as a convenient location was selected and the necessary furnishings provided for the central tool room, all the tools were withdrawn from the local departments, with the exception of a working supply, and a system of eighteen sub or department tool rooms under the direction of the central tool room was established.

Perhaps the easiest way to comprehend intimately the working of this new system is to follow the progress of a tool through the required channels.

In order that there may be no delay in the operations of any workman it is only necessary for him to present a broken or dulled tool at his department sub-tool room to receive immediately a good tool in exchange. It is well at this point to explain that on employment each workman receives from his foreman an order for his initial tool equipment, which he presents to the sub-tool room and receives his tools.

Upon the filling of this requisition the department tool man fills out a card recording the tools in this man's possession and forwards the list to the central tool room, where it is filed. The centralization of these cards makes it possible to insure that each workman will turn in his equipment at the central tool room if he leaves the employ of the company, and final pay is delayed until this is done.

The workman may now break or dull a part of his equipment and require substitutes. These are easily supplied and the injured tools are placed in steel tote baskets of uniform size, broken tools separated from those needing only sharpening or minor repairs. Twice a day a crew of tool room movers call at each department and receive, sorted and packed in tote baskets, the turned-in equipment.

With special trucks which follow a fixed route, the gathering is easily accomplished, and a constant contact is maintained by the central tool room with every outlying station. The tools collected are of every character and include hand and machine tools, portable pneumatic and electric machines, and the rubber boots, gloves and goggles which are furnished for certain occupations.

It is impossible at this point to ignore the lack of similar facilities for the care of the heavy dies, the only feature of an extensive and well-nigh perfect system that is noticeably absent. But it is reasonable to surmise that the future will see this need provided for and a system of electric trucks, cranes and men to move and centralize these weighty but valuable necessities of manufacture installed.

Stuck in each tote box by the man who fills it at the sub-station, is a list of the tools broken or to be sharpened and repaired which have been replaced with effective units. This statement not only describes the tool, but gives the number of the workman who turned it in, information that is often of value in checking up the amount of breakage by individual

KIND OF UNIT Gaskets DESCRIPTION 4" rubber WHEN QUANTITY AVAILABLE FALLS TO 40

BALANCE OF STORES ISSUE ORDER FOR 100

SYMBOL S M-1543
LOCATION IN STORES R-17

INSTRUCTIONS FOR POSTING:
A. WHEN STORES ARE ORDERED, ADD THE QUANTITY TO COLUMNS 1 AND 4
B. WHEN STORES ARRIVE, SUBTRACT THE QUANTITY RECEIVED FROM COLUMN 1 AND ADD THE QUANTITY RECEIVED TO COLUMN 2
C. WHEN STORES ARE APPORTIONED, SUBTRACT QUANTITY FROM COLUMN 4, AND ADD QUANTITY APPORTIONED TO COLUMN 3
D. WHEN STORES ARE ISSUED, SUBTRACT QUANTITY FROM COLUMNS 2 AND 3
NOTE.—IN ALL CASES BRING DOWN AT ONCE BALANCE ON HAND IN EACH COLUMN AFFECTED

1-STORES ORDERED BUT NOT YET RECEIVED						2-STORES ON HAND IN STORE ROOM					3-STORES APPORTIONED TO ORDERS BUT NOT YET ISSUED				4-STORES AVAILABLE THAT IS: ON PURCHASE ORDERS AND ON HAND		
DATE OF REQUISITION	REQUISITION NO.	PURCHASE ORDER NO.	QUANTITY	TOTAL COST	DATE RECEIVED	QUANTITY	DATE ISSUED	ISSUED FOR ORDER NUMBER	TOTAL COST	COST PER UNIT	DATE APPORTIONED	QUANTITY	ORDER NUMBER	DATE ISSUED	DATE	QUANTITY	REMARKS
2/27/10	14521	1728	100		2/20/10	70					[illegible]	20	17216		[illegible]	70	
											[illegible]	15	17349		[illegible]	50	
															[illegible]	35	

The "BALANCE OF STORES" SHEET

This form helps the storekeeper to avoid both overstocking and understocking. The detailed explanation of exactly how to keep the record up to date enables even an inexpensive worker to keep without much trouble a fairly accurate and valuable running account of balances in stock by items

workmen. These tabulations are made monthly and a statement is furnished each department.

On all tools turned in for grinding or repairs the workman signs a ticket on the receipt of new tools. Twice a year a special check is taken from the continuous inventory, and the central lists are checked against the duplicate retained by the sub-tool rooms. The infrequency of a material error marks the efficiency of the system.

But to continue further with the department tool room, let us suppose that the workman now requires additional equipment. Such a tool now becomes a part of the regular equipment and is so reported to headquarters for record. But if a special tool for a special job is required a green tag is required.

Such special tools must be returned each day at closing time and may be taken out again if necessary in the morning. As long as this procedure is followed the green tag, with its information regarding the whereabouts of the tool, remains on a hook in the sub-tool room. But if the tag is not taken up at closing time it automatically proceeds to headquarters and an investigation is made.

In passing, the identification check as a protection against abuse of the system is worth a few words of comment. These tags carry the number of the workman, a number which serves for the gate, identification and tool-room requirements. Should the tag be lost, another bearing the same number, but countersigned with a "2," is issued and a notice of the lost original is posted in the tool room. This automatically outlaws the original check and successfully prevents one workman from securing tools on the check of another.

One more form deserves notice – the employee's tool release. When a workman leaves the employ of the Pullman Company he reports to the paymaster, following a visit to the central tool room, where he turns in his equipment and receives a "tool release" without which, or a sufficient explanation, he will be unable to secure his final pay. From the data already received by the central tool room from the department branch, where he received his initial equipment, it is only a matter of seconds to check off his tools and fill out the release.

There is little at first glance that is impressive about the central tool room.

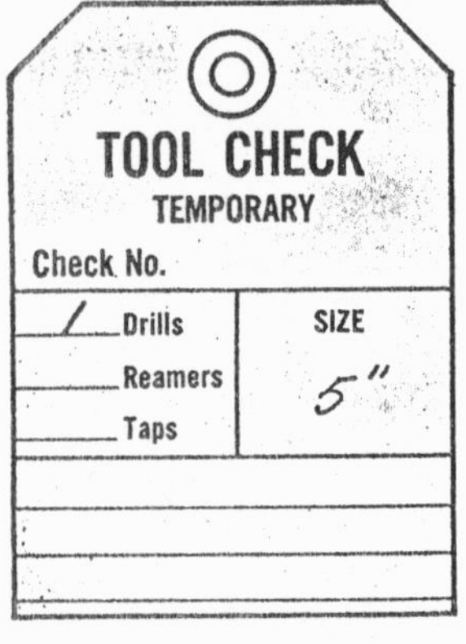

TOOL CHECK
TEMPORARY
Check No.

1 Drills	SIZE
___ Reamers	5"
___ Taps	

The TOOL CHECK

If a special tool is needed, a green tag like this, hanging on a hook in the sub-tool room, always records its exact whereabouts

CHECK NO. 273

QUANTITY WANTED	SYMBOL OF TOOL WANTED
1	L D. 3

DESCRIPTION OF TOOL WANTED

3" Lathe dog

MONTH	DAY	YEAR	SIGNED BY MAN OF ABOVE CHECK NO.
3	29	'16	L. F. Czaritz

NOTE: ONLY ONE KIND OF TOOL CAN BE ISSUED ON THIS CARD, BUT SEVERAL OF THE SAME KIND

The "SPECIAL TOOL" RECEIPT

Special tools are receipted for on a form like this. If the green tag described to the left is not taken up by closing time as a result of the tool being returned, this receipt immediately becomes a valuable acknowledgment of the original issuance of the tool

In one of the older red-brick buildings, almost lost in the maze of surrounding structures, a single room about 50x30 ft. holds this vital center of supply. By the windows in front are the desks of the staff. Behind them four double faced rows of wooden racks stretch back to the far end of the room.

There is a foreman who has charge of the entire department, including the sub-tool rooms. Under him in the central office are a dozen assistants and perhaps twice as many more are required for the sub-tool rooms and the transportation of tools. In the repair department, of which we will speak later, about twenty-five men are employed.

The four great tiers of racks in the central tool room are built on a unit compartment basis, making them readily interchangeable and easily and instantly capable of subdivision into any combination of bins and drawers. The units are square – 24½ by 24½ inches – and a foot and a half deep: great boxes, white painted, piled neatly on their sides with their open tops forming endless rows of shelves.

And each compartment is capable of further subdivision into quarter, eighth, sixteenth or smaller spaces by the introduction of smaller units. In these shelves are gathered a three months' supply of equipment for the entire series of branch departments; a vast collection of drills, reamers, files, punches and dies, taps, threading tools, emery wheels, air and electric portable machinery amd miscellaneous articles, carefully sorted, labeled, inventoried and indexed – a collection valued at $90,000.

If a workman requires a very special tool, such as might not be carried by his department, he comes direct to the central tool room. Here he makes his request, signs a receipt and receives the tool. The tool-room clerk immediately hangs a brass tag bearing the workman's number on a hook outside the compartment from which the man takes the tool and files the receipt. No record can be lost or buried.

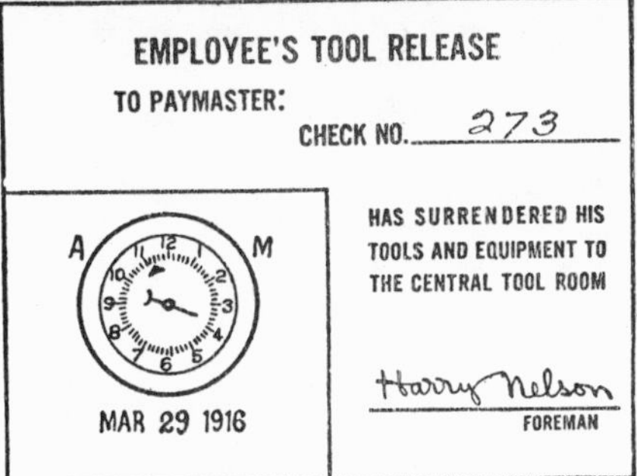

EMPLOYEE'S TOOL RELEASE

TO PAYMASTER:

CHECK NO. 273

A M

MAR 29 1916

HAS SURRENDERED HIS TOOLS AND EQUIPMENT TO THE CENTRAL TOOL ROOM

Harry Nelson

FOREMAN

The "TOOL RELEASE"

When a workman leaves the company he reports to the paymaster, following a visit to the central tool room, where he turns in his complete equipment and quickly receives this "tool release." Without a "tool release" it is of course impossible to secure final pay from the paymaster

Under the direct management of the central tool room comes the repair department, which is housed in the next room and which devotes itself exclusively to tool maintenance and repairs. Here is a purely mechanical department, and its immediate proximity allows the utmost efficiency in the rapid repair of tools requiring expert attention.

Although the Pullman system of centralized tool distribution may appear complicated from this necessary description of details, it requires but brief actual observation to appreciate its marvelous efficiency. Not only is there a saving in materials and tools, but a great reduction has been effected by it in the overhead cost of operations.

Gone are the wasteful days of unskilled grinding, of endless waiting, of long trips to here and there and back again. Today there is well regulated speed and efficiency. There is a record of man and of tool. The careless worker soon marks himself, and as quickly do the records display the weakness of a line of tools or a metal part. Today, when a workman receives his job, his materials are brought to him; he has tools provided necessary for the work. His sole function is to make what is required, and it will be carried away upon the completion of his operation.

Of all the development of the Pullman system, there is none so striking in its physical aspects as this well-groomed method of tool distribution and maintenance. Like the luxurious sleeper, it rolls smoothly, there is no distracting grinding of gears, no jolt or jar; it is truly a fitting example of the perfection of an intelligently conceived and conscientiously followed system of "common-sense management."

The June instalment of this series will take up another important development in modern management which happens to be illustrated in the growth of the Pullman "common-sense" system of management. It is standardization – the development which has reorganized the arrangement of shelves in many little grocery stores, the killing of cattle in the great packing houses, the making of Ford automobiles. And at Pullman standardization guides the making of cars in progressive stages just as it guides the killing of cattle at the packing houses – a pair of trucks grows into a car before your eyes, on one track, in a single building – as you stand watching.

RECORD OF PIECE WORK CONTRACTS ISSUED AND CONDITION OF WORK

TEMPLET NO. 123

CHARGE Frt. Dept.

ARTICLE Coupler Valves

OPERATION M-12-4-				OPERATION				OPERATION				OPERATION				OPERATION				OPERATION			
PIECES	PRICE	PER	AMOUNT	PIECES	PRICE	PER	AMOUNT	PIECES	PRICE	PER	AMOUNT	PIECES	PRICE	PER	AMOUNT	PIECES	PRICE	PER	AMOUNT	PIECES	PRICE	PER	AMOUNT
200	5	1	10.00																				

CARD NO.	CARS COMPLETED	DATE OUT	DATE IN	CARD NO.	CARS COMPLETED	DATE OUT	DATE IN	CARD NO.	CARS COMPLETED	DATE OUT	DATE IN	CARD NO.	CARS COMPLETED	DATE OUT	DATE IN	CARD NO.	CARS COMPLETED	DATE OUT	DATE IN	CARD NO.	CARS COMPLETED	DATE OUT	DATE IN
1721	43	6/22	6/29																				
1830	20	6/24	6/29																				

HOW THE COSTS ARE FIGURED

Payment is made on the piecework basis. The cost and amount of each kind of material needed for each unit of product – a car – is carefully standardized. Then it becomes a simple matter to figure the total material requirements and costs

WHAT A NEW SYSTEM OF MANAGEMENT DID FOR US

Today labor and material costs are rising – and here is a plan that cut payroll charges 25% and losses of materials 50%

Edited by JOHN S. RUNNELLS

By JOSEPH HUSBAND

LABOR and material costs – they are the big problems in many lines now. It's a sellers' market in most cases. Wages are increasing and skilled men hard to get. In some cases wages have increased about 300%. It becomes proportionately important, then, to get the most out of the payroll, to make every ounce of raw material useful. The plan described in this article – worked out by a large concern, it's true, but without doubt applicable in principle to the smallest plant – made it possible for four men to do the work of five. It cut the wastage of material exactly in half. It brought estimates 40% nearer actual costs. Can you afford not to read it carefully?

ONE of the biggest factors in manufacturing today is the idea of logical and practical sequence. Sequence, after all, is but another word for standardization, and standardization is an accepted business gospel.

In the great packing plants the live animals climb by easy inclines to the topmost floor of the packing house, and descending by gravity, pass through the various stages of manufacture until the can of roast beef or the side of lamb arrives at the door of the waiting freight car. All is arranged so that a sequence of stages of manufacture must be observed. No different should be the plan of the smallest manufacturer if he desires to produce goods of quality at a sufficiently low cost to get the business and earn a profit.

Along with sequence comes specialization. The jack-of-all-trades was a handy man in the days before business struck its modern pace, but today the live workman learns to excel at one job and becomes a specialist, and the live employer has learned to break up his manufacture into operations arranged in logical sequence and each performed by one or more of these specialists.

When the Pullman Company some five years ago determined to bring their great manufacturing plant to the point of highest efficiency, scientific management and common sense afforded the means to the desired end. In previous chapters I have described various expressions of that common-sense management: how in the brass department a detailed form of scientific management was found practical and great savings effected by an apparent increase in overhead; how by establishing a central tool room eight thousand workmen received better tools and saved the company hundreds of thousands of dollars in time and material.

And in this article I propose to show how in the great shops where freight cars are built, the Pullman Company has brought about the most economical production by the institution of a system of progressive building, in which the ar-

KEEPING THE WORK MOVING

There are three construction tracks and thirteen standardized positions in the construction of a car. Wagers are freely placed by the men, track against track, position two of track one against position two of track two, and so on down through the positions

The Pullman Company, Manufacturing Department

CONDITION OF WORK IN FREIGHT DEPARTMENT

TO THE SUPERINTENDENT. PULLMAN, ILL., 4—29— 1916

ROAD	LOT NO.	NO. IN LOT	CLASS OF CARS	NO. IN ERECT. SHOP	NO. IN PAINT SHOP AND YARD	TOTAL	LAID OUT		BUILT		SHIPPED	
							TODAY	TOTAL	TODAY	TOTAL	TODAY	TOTAL
F & W.	17136	7	Gondola	2	5	7	1	4	0	3	0	4
C. N & E.	17201	5	Refrigerator	2	0	2	1	3	0	0	0	0
P. & E. L.	17203	10	Gondola	1	6	7	1	9	1	2	0	1

WOOD CONSTRUCTION	TOTAL	STEEL CONSTRUCTION	TOTAL	FORGE AND MACHINE	TOTAL	TOTAL NO. EMPLOYED		TRUCKS			
								LOT	NO. SETS	CLASS	TOTAL
Car Builders	15	Machine	14	Smiths	11	Wood Construction	59	1891	22	80-10	22
Body	15	Construction	26	Machine	20	Steel	74				
Mill Men	12	Hook on	13	Tool	19	Forge and Machine	80				
Air Brakes	4	Labor	21	Labor	30	Labor	122				
Painters	13					Crane	7				
						Miscellaneous	15				
TOTAL	59		74		80		357				

George Snyder GENERAL FOREMAN

WATCHING THE PROGRESS OF THE WORK

From the engineers' specifications, experience quickly figures how many cars can be reasonably expected to be produced in a day. A simple record like this makes it easy to see that production is being held up to standard and to watch progress

ticle manufactured is passed through a sequence of logical stages and emerges completed at the end.

There are so many points of interest in the Pullman system that each can not be specifically described. Few concerns are large enough to adopt so inclusive a system as a whole. But there is no manufacturer who can not profit to his own advantage in some particular instance from the discoveries and experiments in management which this great company has been able to institute, test out, abandon or retain.

Before the days when the old order at Pullman had given place to the new, freight cars were built from the ground up. Like a house or a ship, each was constructed and completed on the spot to which the trucks were first rolled.

To that spot all material was carried. To it came successive workmen to perform their particular work. There was endless hauling, endless wastes of time of the workmen going or coming, and there were wastes of materials beyond computation. As in thousands of other lines of manufacture, no one offered the correction. That was the way cars always had been built; probably the way they always would be. Then came the change.

Today in a great building, so vast that a small village could grow beneath its roof, the Pullman Company manufactures freight cars in a way that has little resemblance to the methods once employed. Today it is the car that moves, and accordingly to the car at definite stages of its manufacture go the materials as needed – up to the limits of the engineer's bill – already prepared as far as possible and assembled for instant incorporation into the car.

At one end of the building a pair of trucks are placed on one of the tracks, down the track they proceed in easy stages, and at each stage or position something is added by workmen who perform no other function. First comes the underframe, further on, the sides, the ends, the roof, and finally from the far end the finished car rolls out into the sunlight. It is nothing more than an evolution of manufacture, a breaking up of operations and the picking out of definite work for specialized men to do.

What has been the result? Although the present system of progressive car building has been in operation less than a year, there has been to date a saving of not less than twenty-five per cent in labor costs alone. And this with the same number of workmen, drawing as high wages as formerly. The answer is that each day the shops are producing more cars than would have been considered possible under the old method.

HERE IS A SAVING WELL WORTH TAKING INTO CONSIDERATION

Again there is the enormous saving in materials. Accurate knowledge of exactly where in the shop each piece of material is to be used, when, how many, by whom, and for what particular car, has ended a condition that once showed a shortage of ten thousand ladder irons at the end of a job, and another time a shortage of one million bolts, all of which had been manufactured and paid for, but had somehow melted in the thin air of an unsystematized organization.

There is always a reasonable unit of disappearance and every plant has its "shop shortage" account, but the Pullman Company discovered that in six months such shortages could be cut fifty per cent by proving that while it may not pay to have the workmen stop to pick up a handful of rivets, it does pay to have some one pick them up for him. At the end of every big job a magnet is passed over the shop floor. Its harvest can be counted in hundreds of dollars.

Probably the first thing that impresses the visitor at the Pullman freight car shops is the logical arrangement of materials and machines, the coherence and sequence of the plant. To the west of the great building and convenient to it, the lumber yard and sheds line the railway spur.

Here are sorted and piled, immediately upon unloading, every piece of timber in such a way that it can be moved in small counted piles without the delay of counting or sorting. South of the lumber yard is the steel yard. Here a crane makes the movement of material simple and rapid.

Following the tracks from the steel yard into the freight car shop the visitor enters at that end of the building which is devoted to steel and wood working machinery, each division occupying the corner nearest to its supply yard outside. The great building is vibrating with the heavy pounding of giant presses, the rattle of riveters, and a thousand other sounds of hammering metal.

In the wood working department there is a roar of band saws and planers. But in spite of the tumult of sound, a curious air of order and system permeates the building. Everything is neatly piled, machines are arranged in orderly groups, and above, rumbling back and forth, giant cranes are lifting and lowering material from one place to another. Nothing lies on the floor. A truck or lift holds each pile, facilitating the orderliness and making it possible for the cranes to pick up the lift and its load as easily as a man picks up his tool kit. If many a small manufacturer would adopt this simple system of standardizing the piling and moving of materials, the saving in time and in lost and damaged materials would soon wipe out the cost of the innovation.

HOW THIS METHOD OF MANUFACTURE IS SCHEDULED AND HANDLED

Beyond the steel and wood shops, parallel tracks extend to the far end of the building and out to the yards beyond. In all there are four tracks, one beneath each great bay, each served by one or more overhead travelling cranes. Of these tracks three are of special interest, for on these three the system of progressive building is conducted.

By analysis, freight car building has been reduced by the Pullman experts to thirteen general operations or positions.

IT PAYS TO MAKE A MAN'S WORK INTERESTING

There is a spirit of rivalry between the thirteen standardized positions on each construction track. The position behind is trying to feed cars to the next position faster than they can be received, while another position may be grumbling that it has finished and is being held up for work. The first six of the thirteen standardized operations or positions in the manufacture of a freight car are indicated above and on page 622

Each operation is sufficiently inclusive to allow for the variations in the manufacture of different types of freight cars. Each position occupies the space of approximately two car lengths, and alongside the track are placed such forges, rivet heaters and other tools as the operation at that position may require.

HOW THE WORK IS KEPT MOVING ACCORDING TO PRODUCTION PLANS

For each position are allotted the men needed to perform the operation, all specialists, of each the proper number. On the other side of the track the various parts to be put in place at this position are assembled, and as far as possible completed from materials delivered by the cranes from the steel and wood shops.

At the first position a gang of fitters fit, ream, and rivet the great steel plates and bars into a giant backbone that rests firmly on the trucks. From the small furnaces the heaters toss to the riveters rivets from carefully counted allotments that have been made for that day's requirements.

A deep whistle blows. The inspectors have reported work completed at each position. Track one is ready to "move." Another whistle in a higher key announces that track two is ready. Far down at the end of the thirteenth position a finished car is pushed out into the yards; at each position the men push up their car to the next position, and to number one is supplied a new pair of trucks.

The first three positions are occupied with the frame of the car, the steel underframe which is to bear the upper body. At the fifth position the sides, built up beside the track ready to attach, are swung into place. At number seven the ends and roof are fastened in position. And so it goes.

In an open space beside the first position the underframe is being drawn together ready to be swung in place on the trucks when the next move is made. To, avoid a waste of time and energy the side frames, at their respective positions, are lowered slowly into a pit while on either side the riveters rivet the plates together as the side frame slowly sinks into the pit. Then it is hoisted and swung into place on the car.

Make a man's work interesting and you have his enthusiasm. When a big order of freight cars comes to the Pullman shops, it is never long before the track rivalry begins and production advances in leaps and bounds.

All three tracks are started at the same minute each morning. At each of the three first positions a pair of trucks mark the first step of the car's growth. Wagers are freely placed, track against track, of position two of track one against position two of track two, and so forth.

The superintendent recalled a big order of several thousand freight cars for a great western road. That took half a year to fill. "Betting day after day, just like teams of ball players. Why, we figure on an average of twenty-one cars for a track a day, and one day competition got so hot they pushed up the record to thirty-three. And," he added, "a man is never too tired at night if there's a spirit of contest in his work."

HOW THIS SUCCESSFUL PLAN MAKES THE WORK INTERESTING

Then, too, there is the spirit of rivalry between positions on the same track. The position behind is trying to feed cars to the next position faster than they can receive them, while another position may be grumbling that they have finished and are being held up for work. It's a game, a game that makes the time move faster and at the same time increases both the workman's pay envelope and the company's production.

Payment is made on the piecework basis. From the engineers' specifications, experience quickly figures how many cars can be reasonably expected to be produced a day.

At the same time what each class of workmen should be entitled to earn per day is figured and the number of men of each class required to produce the cars. Multiply the number of men by the wage and divide by the number of cars and the cost per car is obtained. In this way it becomes possible for every man to profit by each additional car that is made, and at the same time a detailed record is obtained for the accurate determination of costs.

The effectiveness of this system is proved by the fact that today there is less than six per cent variation in the actual cost per car from the engineer's estimate. Formerly a leeway of ten per cent was allowed and this was often exceeded.

The system, moreover, permits an exceedingly simple form of time and material cost keeping. For labor costs all that is need d is the man's name, number, and rate per car. At the end of the day he is credited with the cars that have passed through his position.

In materials all is standardized. Every plate of steel and every rivet that goes to a position goes according to the engineer's specification sheet. There are no wastes, and no losses.

The great value of this Pullman system to the smaller manufacturer lies in the simple application of these great efficiency short cuts to his own business: the arrangement of men and machines in logical sequence, and the determination of the proper number of operators needed at each progressive stage of manufacture in order that the flow of work may be constant and so regulated that almost automatically the finished product will pass to the shipping room hour after hour, day after day, with nowhere along the line a waste of time or materials to cut down the profit.

WHERE SOME OF THE COSTS ARE FIGURED

When the new system of management was introduced, the company frankly admitted that it wanted accurate figures to be used in making estimates

WHAT A NEW SYSTEM OF MANAGEMENT DID FOR US

The rise in the cost of both materials and labor, coupled with the scarcity of good workmen, has set many business men puzzling over an exceedingly complicated problem. They wish to introduce the most thorough-going of time- and cost-keeping systems. They also anticipate that their men may not take to the reforms cheerfully and may become impatient just at a time when a stable working force is most needed. This article tells how a company won the support of its men for a new system of management

By JOHN S. RUNNELLS — *Transcribed by* JOSEPH HUSBAND

IN the preceding instalments of this series have been described the various phases of the system of "common-sense management" which during the past few years has been so successfully installed in the great car manufacturing plant of The Pullman Company.

Drawn in part from other existing plans of scientific management, but in the main originated by The Pullman Company to serve the particular needs of its own requirements, this "system" has thoroughly proved itself, not only by effecting large savings in labor and materials, but by an actual increase in the production of the plant as well as by an attendant increase in the quality of manufacture.

Like so many other great American industries, The Pullman Company was born in a day when scientific management occupied as distant a place on the horizon as the wireless or the phonograph. But within the fifty years that are just now closing, the small car-building company has g own to a size that requires the services of six thousand employees, a small city to contain it, and the world to furnish it the necessary materials for its ramified manufacture.

Every manufacturer, large or small, reaches at least once in his career the moment when he stands face to face with the necessity for a change of methods. The narrow ways that once served, the easy supervision of the small room, the almost personal handling of costs of time and materials, must be abandoned or radically changed. Growth demands systematization. Successful competition requires an exact knowledge of every contributing item – a system must be applied.

But the manufacturer must not for a second feel that a good system can be plastered on his plant like a new roof. Good as the system may be it can succeed only with the cooperation of the workmen. Without their support it must fail utterly.

How to evolve a plan that will be endorsed by the workers and how to present it to them for their support are questions that the individual alone can solve. As a first step, it is necessary always to analyze the new system in order to eliminate any feature that is not fair to the workers. If it is fair, and if it considers the men as intelligent and ambitious individuals, its application is usually simple. The American working man is quick to question an innovation; he is sometimes slow to appreciate the merits of plans or systems that are not immediate in their fulfilment; but when he does realize that mutual, and not selfish, profit will result, he will almost always give his unqualified support.

When a few years ago The Pullman Company evolved its plan for common-sense management, no attempt was made to apply the plan immediately to the entire organization. In certain departments where a reform of system was most needed the application was begun.

In the personal conferences which were necessary between the company and the various foremen in order to outline the new system, the frank admission was made that the purpose of getting things systematized was to obtain accurate figures to be used in estimates. Care was taken that no man should feel in this move any attempt on the part of the company to place the blame for any previous shortcomings.

HOW THE INTEREST OF EMPLOYEES WAS SECURED FOR THE NEW METHODS

It was admitted that there had been many loose ends, but the company took the blame. It was explained that it was unavoidable in building a large number of cars to prevent mistakes which aggregate serious losses, and that the new system was designed to bring the causes for these mistakes to light, not entirely in order to fix responsibility, and by a mutual understanding of the causes to prevent their repetition.

In the late fall of 1912 the plan was begun, and in June of the following year it was well established in several departments. There was no opposition from the employees. Amenable to reason, the men, as soon as they fully understood, took a distinct interest in its development. Very quickly it became recognized that more equitable earnings would result.

The men were better satisfied to be paid for the actual labor they performed than to lose their identity under the former gang system of payment. The older men especially welcomed the change and there was frequently expressed gratification as it became apparent that by the system each man would be paid for what he actually did.

In attempting to reduce time-keeping to an exact science the men have given

IN THE CENTRAL TOOL ROOM

The tools are kept carefully sorted in racks and there is a special method for checking on those which must be returned after the men are through. Instead of sharpening their own tools in a distant tool room, the men receive sharp tools for dull ones at their work places

instantly he has learned to cooperate. So, too, there was once a condition when much material would "disappear" between an operation on one machine and the next. Such disappearances did not necessarily indicate dishonesty. It was charitably regarded a case of unreported spoilage. That such a condition no longer exists comes primarily from the workman's increased personal interest, which is inspired by his realization that the plan of "common-sense" management has made him an individual rather than a mere cog in a turning wheel.

Suggestions for improvements from the men have greatly increased, and while the majority are apt to prove impractical or applicable only to some one job which may be performed under individual conditions, yet a number of excellent short cuts and savings have come from them. Suggestions for such improvements of manufacture are paid for in money if they find approval in the eyes of the company's Committee on Standards.

It is only natural that an orderly and intelligent system should enable the workmen to produce individually in greater volume. It is also quite natural that a man might occasionally feel that because he was producing more, that by that much he must be working harder. As a matter of fact, the system has actually lightened labor and the men have invariably sooner or later realized the change.

No longer is it necessary for the workman to seek and carry his materials, or

their fullest cooperation and there is nothing to indicate that any man has quit because of it. Likewise, effort is made to induce the workmen promptly to report mistakes and let the management remedy the difficulty.

In former years the bad condition of a tool or a machine would often entail heavy spoilage before it was discovered. Today the workman reports the condition

sharpen his tools in a distant tool room. Materials are delivered at his machine as he requires them, tools are sharpened or replaced by new. Undisturbed he is permitted to devote his energies to production, and by increasing his production to find additional compensation in his increased earning capacity.

Due to the fact that the application of the system has placed in the company's hands accurate cost figures, it has become possible for the company to bid more closely, and accordingly secure more car business, to the ultimate increase of manufacture and the workmen's immediate benefit.

Whenever a change is made in a department, and a better system for handling any part or all of the work is required, the department foremen and leaders are called into the general office. The proposed plan is then described with careful detail and every man has an opportunity to ask questions or make suggestions.

So fully are details thrashed out that from these meetings a finished plan is usually produced. As soon as the plan is ready for application the foremen in turn explain the innovation to their men. In this way the foremen act as the personal link between the general office and these men, and greater frankness of discussion is made possible.

An interesting feature of the Pullman system of management is the fact that it has put into the men's hands the means to communicate immediately with the company regarding the performance of their work. Foremen's meetings are occasionally held for an interchange of ideas. Working as individuals there is no shifting of responsibility, and there is today at Pullman the desire on the part of the workmen to correct rather than tacitly accept.

Combined with a plan as comprehensive as the Pullman system is necessarily

SIMPLE BUT EFFECTIVE

Each man has a numbered piece of brass which he receives as he passes into the yard and which he hangs over the proper square in a box like this when he reaches the section of the plant in which he works. The brass pieces are deposited at the gate by the men as they leave

a department devoted to the welfare of the men. Here there are probably no particularly striking innovations, but the thoroughness of the work undertaken demands at least passing comment. Free medical advice and treatment, not only to the injured but to the sick, are afforded. A dispensary thoroughly equipped, and with many of the advantages of a hospital, is in charge of a nurse and two physicians and an ambulance is maintained for use in case an emergency arises.

Such features are not unalloyed altruism; they are the commom-sense features of a common-sense management. No manufacturer can neglect the health of his employees; the direct return is better work. The greater loyalty which comes from proper sanitary precautions and medical assistance is of far greater value than the investment involved.

Further cooperation is given to men employed in special lines of work. To the painters and lead and acid workers overalls are supplied and kept in repair. Goggles are provided for men doing work in which there is the liability of eye injury.

Further, a corps of approximately six men are almost constantly engaged in looking after the safety devices for the machines. Injury has been reduced to a minimum.

One big lesson to be drawn from the application of the Pullman plan of "common-sense" management is that no improvements are possible without the employee's cooperation. The materials, the machines, the plan, all may be yours, but the question of the success of it all is the workman's – without his cooperation the best devised plan must fail. With his cooperation "common-sense" management can usually be made to bring to any manufacturer an added profit and to the workman a more congenial employment and an increased wage.

ONE RESULT OF WINNING THE WORKMAN'S COOPERATION

In former years the bad condition of a machine would often entail heavy spoilage before it was discovered. Today the workman reports the condition instantly – he has learned to cooperate

SCIENTIFIC MANAGEMENT IN A RETAIL STORE

C. Bertrand Thompson

The vice-president of a precedent-making store sums up Mr. Thompson's articles in this way:

With his philosophy I am in general agreement. The system of expense classification which he proposes is somewhat different from that we employ, being rather more elaborate in some respects and less elaborate in others; but this does not signify anything more than the possibility that neither Mr. Thompson nor we may be entirely right. It is certain that retail distributers, both large and small, can find suggestions in Mr. Thompson's article that, if brought to careful application by them, would result in considerable savings and improved profits through increased efficiency in management.

SCIENTIFIC MANAGEMENT

IN A RETAIL STORE

I

How the principles proved in factories can be applied by merchants

By C. BERTRAND THOMPSON *Illustrated with* PHOTOGRAPHS *and* DIAGRAMS

RUNNING a retail store by scientific management is an idea quite new to store managers. They have heard of scientific management and the possibility of its application to railroads, and they know that factories and a few government establishments are being operated under scientific management. The popular idea of this particular development is that it consists in the application of stopwatches and motion study to the work of operatives and the administration of a factory with an excessive amount of red tape.

One would not have to reflect long, however, to arrive at the conclusion that, if this is all scientific management consisted of, it would have died a natural death long ago, instead of being, as it is, the livest issue in modern industrial developments. Scientific management includes time study and motion study and an elaborate number of forms and records which naturally gives the appearance of red tape. But these things do not constitute the system; they are merely parts of the mechanism. The system itself consists of a series of principles whose application, as made by Fred W. Taylor and his group of engineers, is but one particular form. The mechanism is in many cases not adaptable to retailing, but the principles are.

Anyone familiar with the fine arts is thoroughly used to the idea of transferring the principles of one art to another. Take the principle of contrast, for example, originating probably in dramatic literature, where the interplay of opposing characters stimulated a pleasurable interest. This same principle of contrast was extended to architecture and sculpture and later to painting, and in modern times to music.

The aim sought in any fine art is the same in all of them. They give an æsthetic pleasure, which suggests that the means successful in one would probably be successful in another; and experience has justified this supposition.

It is reasonable to suppose that the same principle would apply to the art of management, whether it is management of a factory or a store. In both cases the end to be gained is the same, the production of a utility at the lowest cost. In the case of a factory the utility takes the form of a change in the shape and condition of the materials handled; they go in, for instance, as bales of cotton and come out as bolts of cloth. The thing produced is the change in form. In a store the product is also a utility, but a utility of location. The goods arrive in packages at the store, where they are wanted only for distribution, and are sold in units to the customer who wants them for use. The only change they have experienced is the change in location; but as this is a useful change, it is a utility, exactly as the change in form made by the factory.

Besides producing the same thing, utilities, both factory and store make use of the same producing factors—men, materials, equipment, and buildings. Instead, therefore, of its being difficult to see how the principles of factory management can apply to store management, it is rather more difficult to see how they can fail to apply.

The fundamental principles of scientific management as practiced in industrial establishments are: first, the organization of the present scattered knowledge in regard to the business into a coherent science; and, second, the organization of the human and material factors involved to secure the most efficient application of the science.

That there is a science of production has been known to engineers and factory managers for decades; and that this science includes not merely the chemistry and physics of engineering, but the technique of machine operation and hand work has been demonstrated for years under scientific management. As Mr. Taylor has shown, there is a science of shoveling as well as a science of bridge building—simpler, of course, but none the less ascertainable and definite. There is a science of selling, too, and many people are trying to find out what it is, thus recognizing

NOTE

SCIENTIFIC management subdivides mechanical and routine operations from planning or mental operations according to certain definite rules. Up to the present time, this particular system of management has been confined to industrial operations, chiefly to factories.

In developing a system of scientific management for factory work Frederick W. Taylor laid down five principles which have stood the test under a variety of conditions and which have given rise to a "school of management." Mr. Thompson belongs to this group of managers and speaks with the authority of an exact knowledge of the Taylor system and of a practical experience in reorganizing factory work.

This article explains how certain of the Taylor principles have been applied in a retail store. The editors of SYSTEM believe that this is the first time the principles of "scientific management" as worked out in a factory, have been applied in a retail store.

In this first article Mr. Thompson reviews the five principles and shows how they may be applied as a group. He also points out that in many stores some of the methods he will describe in greater detail in later articles have been used in other forms and under other names.

Aside from the definite methods for securing better results which the series will bring out, the articles as a whole comprise a distinct contribution to the growing volume of literature on scientific management, and make clear once more that business principles and methods are transferable from one class of business to another.

the application of this manufacturing principle to marketing.

The principal methods in a scientifically managed factory for securing proper organization of the human and material factors include: first, the selection of the right men for the job; second, the systematic training of each man for his job and for transfer to other jobs when needed; third, an accurate determination of a definite quantity and quality of work which each man may reasonably be expected to produce, day in and day out, without inconvenience; fourth, the establishment of such conditions as will in every way facilitate the work of the operator, such as careful planning of all work in advance and having on hand at the machine or work place all the materials, tools, and instructions necessary for the workman to proceed; fifth, the payment of a wage sufficiently above the ordinary to be an inducement to the workman to accept the instruction and other facilities offered him.

Some of these methods are already familiar to store and sales managers and have been consciously developed, in some cases to a high degree of perfection.

Though it cannot be said that the selection of sales people, buyers, and the force of help about a store, is done on any noticeably scientific basis, it is evident that considerable thought has been given to the training of such people as are actually employed. Classes in salesmanship are quite common. Committee meetings of buyers, and so on, practically amount to the same thing; and frequent conferences between the heads of a concern and their subordinates are in many stores the occasion of definite instruction. Conventions of salesmen are utilized for the same purpose. Thus the second method has secured considerable recognition.

The establishment of a quota of sales, whether as the basis for the tenure of a job or the fixing of a salary, is a recognition of the third method: the establishment of a definite task.

A CLASS IN RETAIL SELLING METHODS. THE STUDENTS ARE ALL NEW EMPLOYEES, THE INSTRUCTOR A PROFICIENT SALESWOMAN, AND THE CUSTOMER HAS REALLY COME TO BUY

THE FIVE PRINCIPLES OF MANAGEMENT, SHOWN ON THIS AND THE FOLLOWING TWO PAGES, HAVE BEEN LAID DOWN FOR FACTORIES AND HAVE APPARENT APPLICATION IN RETAIL STORES

Fixing the salary proportionally to the sales made, whether in the form of commission, bonus, premium, or what not, is in a degree a recognition of the fifth method—I say "in a degree" because the increased compensation in selling is usually paid simply for the product; that is, the quantity of sales and not, as in factories operating under scientific management, for the acceptance of instruction and increased facilities provided by the management, which brings with it as a by-product an increase in output. Commission and premium schemes as applied to sales are more like the old piece rate system in factories. In the piece rate system someone sets a rate according to his judgment, and the worker is paid exactly in proportion to the number of pieces produced. The management does nothing in particular to assist him in production, but depends on the operator's initiative and ability to devise improvements and increase his output. This is evidently entirely different from the method of scientific management, which has standardized so far as possible all the conditions under which the operator works, trains him thoroughly to the best use of the conditions provided, sets a task based upon the continuance of such conditions, and pays a high rate for their acceptance.

It should be clear from this comparison that the feature in which sales management is most undeveloped in comparison with factory management is in the organization of the conditions in which the work is done. In other words, in the adequate performance of the duties which should devolve upon the management and which affect sales only indirectly. Take the stock-handling system of any large department store as an example. The store gives the best of its attention and ability to advertising, to the selection of buyers and the training of salespeople;

I *The* SELECTION *of* EMPLOYEES

"THE selection of the right employee for the job" has been carried further in many retail stores than in factories. There is still opportunity of more scientific selection

but its store and stock-rooms are usually inadequate, poorly lighted, poorly located, poorly accounted for, and in general, in comparison with the factory storeroom, quite inefficiently managed. The expense connected with the management of a storeroom is charged as "non-productive" or "burden" and the idea, now becoming obsolete in factory management, that overhead or indirect expense is a burden and therefore to be reduced to a minimum, still prevails largely in marketing.

The same observations apply to the usual retail accounting systems. They are looked upon as a necessary evil. As much attention as is necessary is given to the commercial accounts—those by which the manager keeps posted on how much he owes and how much is owing to him. But of cost accounting, as that term is known to the factory manager, there is little or nothing; and yet it is reasonable to suppose that the same methods of cost accounting which have fully demonstrated their value in manufacturing might be at least equally useful if applied to selling.

It is the object of the articles in this series to point out how these two features

II *The* TRAINING *of* EMPLOYEES

"THE systematic training of employees for their tasks" is carried out by sales classes and special instructors in many large stores

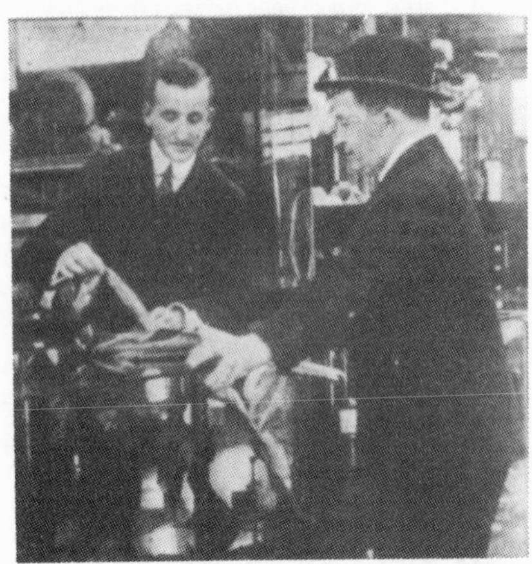

III STANDARDIZING *the* TASK

"THE determination of just the amount of work an employee can do in a day" has more variables in store than in factory but offers a field for scientific study

of management are handled: how cost accounting and the accounting for materials received, handled, and delivered, may be successfully transplanted from factories to stores. And it may not be superfluous to add that the articles are really an account of what the writer has already successfully accomplished.

Most department stores and large retail establishments have developed certain parts of their system to a high degree of perfection. The most immediate and important problem that they have is to buy the right goods at the right time, to get them before the customer and sell them as quickly as possible at a profit. The very life of the organization depends on the satisfactory solution of this problem; consequently, it has received the greatest share of attention and has been in many cases satisfactorily worked out. The buyers are carefully selected, well trained, closely checked, and highly rewarded. Dealings with manufacturers and sources of supply have been reduced to a science, until the manufacturers, especially the smaller ones, have become almost universally at the mercy of the large retailer, especially in respect to the making and storage of goods until called for, so that the manufacturer bears the burden of investment in stock which a few years ago was borne by the retailer. Advertising and display have similarly been highly developed, until the appeal of "special bargains," "quality," and "service" has become well nigh irresistible. Schools have been installed and instructors retained to teach the salespeople the best method of closing with the customer. In short, some of the fundamental principles of what is known among manufacturers as scientific management have for some time been applied—in a more or less unconscious and haphazard way, to be sure—to retailing.

This situation is analogous to that which existed in industrial activities several years ago when the technique of production was receiving the lion's share of attention. The manufacturer considered that he existed to make the product and that his chief problem was to make it as quickly and as cheaply as possible. The product was apparently made "at the point of the tool" and it was therefore the technique of machinery, equipment and material that got his attention. It was at least twenty-years ago, however, that manufacturers

IV PLANNING *the* WORK

"THE planning of general conditions to facilitate selling" has already been analyzed in many stores. A more scientific approach is possible in many cases

V *The* PAYMENT *of* EMPLOYEES

"WAGES as an incentive to meet quotas of work" – loosely applied in retailing as bonuses. Much more can be done to determine basis for payment

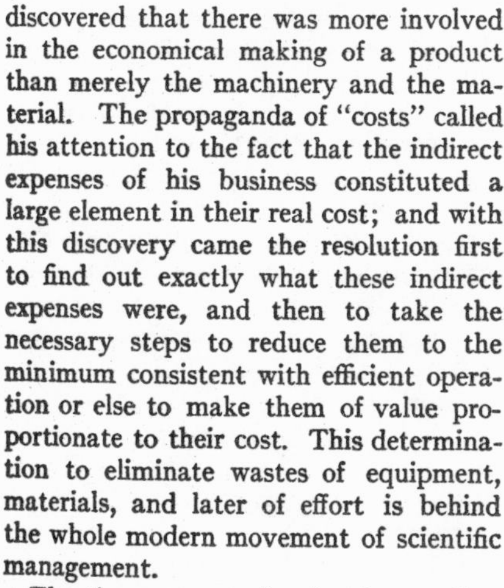

discovered that there was more involved in the economical making of a product than merely the machinery and the material. The propaganda of "costs" called his attention to the fact that the indirect expenses of his business constituted a large element in their real cost; and with this discovery came the resolution first to find out exactly what these indirect expenses were, and then to take the necessary steps to reduce them to the minimum consistent with efficient operation or else to make them of value proportionate to their cost. This determination to eliminate wastes of equipment, materials, and later of effort is behind the whole modern movement of scientific management.

The time seems to be ripe for retailers to pursue the same course. Nothing is more striking to the student of industrial methods than the co-existence in the same store of the most refined methods of buying, advertising, and selling, with the very crudest methods of receiving, storing, handling, and delivery of goods, and the most cumbersome methods of accounting. The relatively greater profits in retailing—or perhaps the ignorance of the retailer as to the real extent of his profits—have succeeded in covering up the necessity for close supervision and the importance of detail. Retail merchants, however, are already bitten with the cost germ and are discovering that their profits are not quite what they thought they were. Or else they have begun to take a pride in the efficient management of their business for the sheer artistic satisfaction that comes from doing a thing exactly right, and they appear to be at least in a receptive attitude toward scientific management.

As the store manager reads this and reflects on the great mass of printed forms, running into the hundreds, which he uses, he may wonder what these statements mean. It looks to him as though, if his store has anything, it certainly has system. It undoubtedly does have system of the type familiar to manufacturers fifteen years ago: that is, numerous and variegated cards and sheets, expensively ruled and highly colored. It is the very quantity and complexity of these forms and the clumsiness of their use which open him to the charge of wastefulness. Retail merchants should see what manufacturers have long since discovered that efficient system does not consist in a multiplicity of forms, but in the quick, accurate, and economic securing of valuable results in the way of useful information in regard to the business, and more particularly in the reduction of wasted effort.

The extent of antiquated methods in the administration of retail establishments as revealed by recent investigations would almost lead one to question whether store managers are anywhere near ready for any form of scientific management. One gains reassurance, however, from the readiness with which shoe retailers are accepting and installing the uniform cost accounting system developed and provided for them by the Harvard University Bureau of Business Research. Reports from all over the country indicate that this system is not only being adopted bodily by leading shoe retailers but is also influencing the accounting system and business methods of many more. This cost system should lead retailers, as similar systems led manutacturers, to take the next step, which is to reduce the costs of doing business as soon as those costs are accurately ascertained.

As I have pointed out in former articles,* the beginning of wisdom is analysis and classification. A classification once made is exceedingly useful and pays for itself many times over, as will be shown later. But even more valuable than the classification is the detailed analysis of the business which is necessary before classification can be begun. Before you can classify your costs, you must know exactly, exhaustively, and in minute detail what you are spending your money for; and the mere gathering of this information and putting it down on paper is in itself a startling eye-opener.

Probably the first thing it will show is that from twice to five times more blanks and forms are being used than are necessary, and that, with proper management, the clerical force can be considerably reduced and quicker and more accurate results secured. It will also undoubtedly show, in a fairly large store, that the stock of supplies of various sorts, such as wrapping paper, twine, elevator supplies, janitor's supplies, and so on, is a considerable but indefinite quantity, scattered all over the place, and subject to no direct control whatever.

If the store runs a soda fountain or a restaurant, an analysis of costs will probably show first that they (or at least the restaurant) do not pay; and an analysis of supplies will probably show a variety of brands and of prices and a laxity of control which may account largely for the deficit.

You undoubtedly have, or can easily get, a sufficiently good system of accounting for your merchandise. You know from your inventory the billed prices of your purchases, the freight and cartage on them, and the discounts. It is not so safe to wager that you know or can get easily the depreciation on your stock or the cost of returned goods in the course of a year; but even this you may have. If you are right up to the minute, you know the cost of heat, light, power, repairs and renewals of equipment, depreciation of equipment, office supplies and expenses; and of course it is easy to get your rent, insurance, taxes and licenses, and management of office salaries. If you are running a small store as a unit, you can know, with this information in hand, whether you are making a profit. But if your store is departmentalized even to the slightest extent, it is reasonably certain that the indirect expenses are not being apportioned properly over your departments and, consequently, that you cannot tell which departments are running at a profit or at a loss and how much the profit or loss is per department. For you must remember that the mere accounting for merchandise does not give you this information. Your merchandise accounts may show a profit for a department which is in fact entirely wiped out by a proper apportionment of your indirect expenses; and it is precisely this indi-

* The earlier articles to which Mr. Thompson refers will be found in SYSTEM for September, October and December, 1912, and January, February, March and April, 1913.

rect expense which store managers as a rule know little or nothing about.

The analysis and classification of costs which I shall describe is intended to make it easy to determine the exact amount of indirect as well as direct cost and to provide a quick and easy method of apportionment of the indirect over the direct cost. It is not an easy and simple matter to make the analysis and classification. On the contrary, it calls for a great deal of thought and painstaking care. But as usual, thorough planning means easy application; and that such is the case with this analysis and classification has been demonstrated. Applied to an up-to-date department store in which the manager got each month, from twenty to thirty days after the end of the month, an accurate distribution sheet, its first result was to get the distribution sheet five days after the end of the first month, and three days after the end of the second. It is now used to get a *weekly* distribution sheet laid on the maager's desk the first thing Monday morning.

For what kind of things does a store pay out its cash? In the first place, of course, it pays salaries and its bills for merchandise, and in most cases rent, and interest on borrowed money. In addition it has many bills for freight, express and cartage, advertising, office supplies, wrappings and delivery expense, insurance and taxes, repairs and renewals of equipment. In addition to these actual expenditures, the store should have a proper charge for depreciation on stock and on fixtures. There will be many other items of expense such as telephone and telegraph, elevators, janitor service, stock handling, and so on, and in some large stores there may be such adjuncts as an employment department, an information bureau, waiting rooms, and perhaps even a bank.

This does not exhaust the list by any means. Every store has an accounting department more or less developed, and occasionally has to meet legal expenses and to pay for protection against theft. One of its largest items is likely to be for advertising, including primarily newspapers, window dressing, catalogs, and billboards, and extending into a wide variety of special advertising accounts, such as contributions to charities, fairs, and so on, dodgers, circular letters, programs, magazines, and gifts, such as playing-cards, fans, rulers, pencils, and so on, inscribed with the name of the concern.

To illustrate in further detail, the advertising department may employ special men of its own, requiring salaries and wages; there will be certain telephone and telegraph charges against this department alone; it will consume a considerable quantity of supplies and stationery, and in some cases may even maintain a small printing plant to set up large newspaper advertisements in advance.

All these items and more need to be analyzed and classified. The procedure will be explained in a second article.

MR. THOMPSON'S *second article will show how this detail classification of accounts was carried out in a medium-sized department store. A third article makes clear how the indirect expenses of merchandising, so classified, can be distributed to their different departments, and the fourth and concluding article will describe the principles and methods of keeping track of stock.*

Of these methods the store's owner, who prefers not to be identified, says, "In the olden days if I asked the office for the distribution of the previous month's expenses, the reply was, 'we'll give it to you in a few days.' Now I get the figures at the end of each month"

TWO years ago, SYSTEM published three articles on the principles of adapting "mnemonic" (easy to remember) symbols for classification. The president of the retail store who read these articles adopted the plan in his store. Here is his letter concerning the classification of his business which Mr. Thompson describes in detail in this and two articles to follow. The editors of SYSTEM belie e that this is the first published account of a definite plan for applying "scientific management" in a retail store

"WE have been using this mnemonic system of symbols in our store for several years. It did not take more than thirty days' use of this system to show us its value.

"I feel that the mnemonic system as applied to the department store, especially in the handling and distribution of its expenses, is very satisfactory. It gives information which the manager of every department store should have constantly at his fingers' ends, together with the totals at various periods. The periods, of course, would vary in length according to the size of the business. In our case we call a month a period, but I can see where in a larger concern the periods could be made shorter – semi-monthly, weekly, or even daily if necessary.

"In the olden days, if I asked the office for certain information, such as the distribution of the previous month's expenses, the reply was

SCIENTIFIC MANAGEMENT

IN A RETAIL STORE

II

How to Make a Basic Expense Classification

By C. BERTRAND THOMPSON — *With an* ILLUSTRATIVE CHART

THE first principle of scientific management, you remember, is the organization of scattered knowledge into a systematized whole. Suppose we apply this principle to our accounts. Fortunately we can do this easily by the application of precisely the method which is used in developing a complete system of accounts for a factory, making of course such changes in the terminology as are obviously necessary.

The first thing to do is to list every item of expenditure that there is a record of—and there should be a record of every expenditure made. When this is accomplished, the next thing to do is to classify these items into a few very broad groups. This classification may be made by the aid of the following questions:

First question: Is the expenditure for materials or work to be sold? If the answer is Yes, it may be classified as an expenditure for merchandise or products to be sold as merchandise, such as the meals served in a restaurant. Such expenditure is direct cost; and as all

usually, 'We will give it to you in a few days.' Those few days usually extended to four or five weeks, and meantime the ship had ample time to find a rock. Now, I have placed before me, directly after the last of each month, every expense of this store with comparisons of previous years. I receive this information promptly and can make all manner of comparisons without the nightmare known as 'incidentals and sundries' of which most auditors seem to approve.

"The added expense of gathering this information is almost microscopic and when I look back to the time when I had to wait for our office to look up this vital information, I am astonished that something of this nature had not been worked out before. These methods are to be gradually applied to all the different departments in our store."

—*From the President of a Department Store.*

DEPARTMENT store officials who have read this series in proof agree that the principles of "scientific management" which Mr. Thompson laid down in the first article may be widely applied. The writer of this letter indicates that at least one section of such a scheme of management has been applied successfully. It should not be overlooked that the departmentalizing of accounts may be carried out by other methods than that of mnemonic symbols proved most valuable in "scientific management"

other expenditures (except capital expenditures, such as permanent additions to land and buildings and equipment) are to be reckoned as a percentage of the selling price of the merchandise, all others are indirect.

If the expenditure is for materials or work not to be sold directly, a second question is in order: Does the material or work increase the permanent value of the store?

If the expenditure is for fixtures, machinery and equipment (except for that which is to be written off immediately when purchased) or for land and buildings, it should be classified as a capital account. If it is not for such items, nor for material or work to be sold, it is chargeable to some kind of indirect expense.

In the latter case there should be asked the third question: Can the expenditure be charged directly to a department? All expenditures which can be, should be classified at once as departmental expenses.

And in regard to those which cannot be charged directly to a department, the fourth question is in order: Is the expense for direct handling of merchandise or dealing with customers? If it is, it may be classified as an auxiliary expense; and if it is not, then as an administrative expense.

The dividing line between auxiliary and administrative expense is somewhat shadowy; and in some cases it is immaterial which way the expense is classified, provided the classification, once made, is consistently adhered to. It has a certain usefulness, however, inasmuch as auxiliary expenses are by definition those which are necessary for the proper handling of goods and customers, and in case of retrenchment, therefore, these should be the last to be attacked. Administrative expenses, on the other hand, though necessary to the successful management of the business, may in many cases be cut down, at least temporarily, without serious harm.

An intelligent answering of these questions would result in a workable classification of every item of expenditure.

Adhering to the mnemonic system of symbols used in scientific management and illustrated in former articles in this magazine, suppose that we make a base sheet for our major classification which will read as follows:

A Auxiliary
B Administrative
D Departmental
M Merchandise
(S Stores and supplies)
Y Fixtures and sprinkler system
*Z Land and buildings

Subdividing now our main base sheet, let us see what the classification will be in a typical, moderate-sized department store.

The Auxiliary Expenses will be listed and symbolized as follows:

AA Advertising
AC Cash system
AE Elevators
AF Telephone and telegraph
AH Heat, light and power not elsewhere classified
AJ Janitor service
AK Stock-room
AL Alterations and repairs
AM Employment
AN Information bureau and post office
AP Shipping department
AR Receiving department
AS Supply department
AT Transportation
AW Waiting room
AZ Land and buildings: repairs, maintenance and rent

The base sheet for Administrative Expense will be this:

BA Accounting department
BE Educational department
BF Floorwalkers
BG General offices
BH Shopping
BL Legal expenses
BM Mail order department
BN Insurance
BP Protection
BS Statistical department
BV Inventories
BX Taxes
BY System expenses

D is the general symbol for Departmental Expense and, where there are but few departments, a letter may be added after the D to symbolize the department: for instance, in a shoe store that is divided into men's, women's, infants', and hosiery departments, these will be designated as DM, DW, DN (I and O are omitted from this symbolic system on account of their resemblance to the figures 1 and 0), and DH, respectively. In a department store this is not practicable without classifying and symbolizing the departments with a resultant symbol of two or three letters for each one. In order, therefore, to keep the symbols short, it is better to number the departments; and this number should be inserted immediately after the D. In the following base sheet for Departmental Expenses, the dash after the D is for the symbol or number of the department:

D-A Advertising for special departments
D-B Buying
D-C Repairs and maintenance
D-E Equipment
D-H Handling cash and goods
D-K Marking
D-L Alterations
D-S Selling
D-T Transportation

It will be noted that in the original base sheet, S is included in parenthesis, as is also M; this is for the purpose of reserving these symbols for materials constituting stores and supplies and for merchandise.

The classifications of fixtures and of land and buildings are simple and obvious and, as they do not enter into our expense account, except as to depreciation which is otherwise charged, their base sheets are not given here.

A few typical base sheets for detailed classes of expenditure may be given as guides to the development of a complete classification—for instance:

AA Advertising

AAA Salaries and wages, except window-dressers
AAB Billboards
AAC Contributions
AAF Telephone (toll) and telegraph
AAG Catalogs
AAJ Dodgers
AAL Circular letters
AAM Magazines
AAN Newspapers—AA1N, —AA2N, —AA3N
AAP Programs
AAR Reclamation of errors
AAS Supplies and stationery, except for window-dressing

*In practice in making up a classification, it is desirable invariably to put down all the letters of the alphabet, omitting "I" and "O." Letters not used are omitted here and elsewhere in this article from considerations of space.

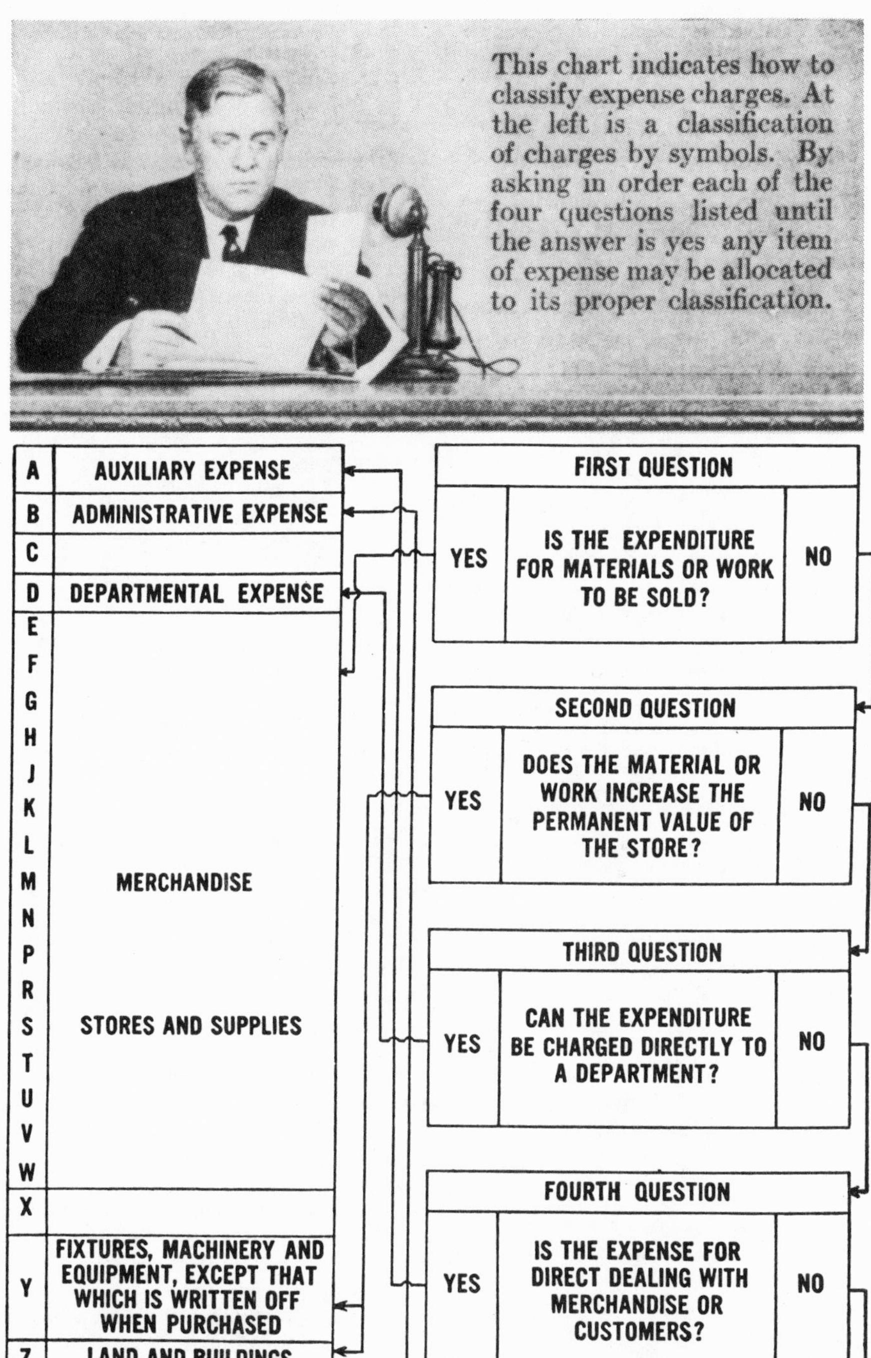
This chart indicates how to classify expense charges. At the left is a classification of charges by symbols. By asking in order each of the four questions listed until the answer is yes any item of expense may be allocated to its proper classification.
A AUXILIARY EXPENSE
B ADMINISTRATIVE EXPENSE
C
D DEPARTMENTAL EXPENSE
E
F
G
H
J
K
L
M MERCHANDISE
N
P
R
S STORES AND SUPPLIES
T
U
V
W
X
Y FIXTURES, MACHINERY AND EQUIPMENT, EXCEPT THAT WHICH IS WRITTEN OFF WHEN PURCHASED
Z LAND AND BUILDINGS
FIRST QUESTION
YES
IS THE EXPENDITURE FOR MATERIALS OR WORK TO BE SOLD?
NO
SECOND QUESTION
YES
DOES THE MATERIAL OR WORK INCREASE THE PERMANENT VALUE OF THE STORE?
NO
THIRD QUESTION
YES
CAN THE EXPENDITURE BE CHARGED DIRECTLY TO A DEPARTMENT?
NO
FOURTH QUESTION
YES
IS THE EXPENSE FOR DIRECT DEALING WITH MERCHANDISE OR CUSTOMERS?
NO

AAV Advertising mediums not elsewhere classified
AAW Window-dressing

Under AAN, you will notice AA1N, AA2N, and so on. These are the symbols for the specific newspapers advertised in.

You will also notice an account, AAR, reclamation of errors. This is for such charges as arise out of mistakes made by the advertising department of which it is desirable to keep a separate account. The same application should be made to the work of every department.

AAW, window-dressing, may be subdivided thus:

AAWA Salaries and wages
AAWC Repairs and maintenance
AAWE Equipment
AAWR Reclamation of errors
AAWS Supplies and stationery

An important classification in some stores will be that of AH, heat, light and power, not elsewhere classified. It will cover the following items:

AHA Salaries and wages
AHB Repairs and maintenance for boilers, engines and other machinery, not elsewhere classified
AHC Repairs and maintenance for fixtures and furniture, not elsewhere classified.
AHE Equipment
AHF Fuel
AHL Electricity
AHP Repairs and maintenance for piping, fixtures and wiring
AHS Stores and supplies and stationery

Alterations and repairs should have an account of their own, for which we would use this base sheet:

ALA Salaries and wages
ALC Repairs and maintenance
ALE Equipment
ALM Materials
ALR Reclamation of errors
ALS Supplies and stationery, not elsewhere classified

Alterations and repairs and rent for land and buildings are symbolized respectively AZC and AZR.

General office expenses, which may amount to a considerable item, may be grouped in this way:

BGA Salaries and wages
BGB Books and periodicals
BGC Repairs and maintenance
BGD Dues and assessments in associations
BGE Equipment
BGF Telephone (tolls) and telegrams
BGN Entertainment
BGS Supplies and stationery
BGT Traveling

Insurance is taken care of as follows:

BNB Bonds
BNC Repairs and maintenance of sprinkler system
BNL Liability
BNS Stock and fixtures

Buying expenses are sometimes important and heavy. They should be grouped in accordance with the following base sheet:

D-BA Salaries and wages
D-BB Bonuses
D-BC Commissions
D-BE Extra premiums
D-BF Telephone (tolls) and telegrams
D-BN Entertainment
D-BR Reclamation of errors
D-BS Supplies and stationery
D-BT Traveling
D-BX Loss on sales (mark-downs)

This buying expense classification is based upon a fairly highly developed organization in which it is possible easily to segregate most of the expenses. It can be applied to smaller organizations, however, by a reasonable apportionment of expenses between the classifications concerned. For instance, if the same individual is engaged in both buying and selling, it ought not to be difficult to charge part of his salary to one, and part to the other. Do not be misled into thinking there are no buying expenses because you may not happen to have buyers so-called; nor, on the other hand, into thinking that all the expenses of a buyer, and especially in a department store, are buying expenses. If a manager in a small store sells goods, keeps the accounts, and does the buying, part of his salary should be charged to buying, even though he performs that function nights and Sundays. On the other hand, in a department store where the buyer is the head of the department and may also do some selling, care should be taken to charge to buying expenses only that part of his time which is actually occupied in buying. This calls for the exercise of judgment and cannot be absolutely accurate, but it can easily be made accurate enough for ordinary purposes.

The degree of minuteness to which this classification will be carried will vary of course with the relative importance of the department or function under consideration. For instance, if the mail order department is a considerable part of the business, it will have a complete classification of expenses of its own; while if it is distinctly subsidiary, a much rougher and less complete classification will serve.

In the apportionment to each function of a business of such items as supplies, it becomes necessary to organize a supply department, from which supplies are issued to other departments on requisition, which may be charged directly against the department receiving them. Here again successful factory experience has been easily transplanted to department store work. The best way of handling this is to gather the supplies and stationery into a storeroom, make it someone's business to act as storekeeper, and classify and otherwise handle the supplies as suggested in my former article, "Listing Stock to Index Wastes," which appeared in the March, 1913, number of SYSTEM.

HOW INDIRECT EXPENSES ARE CORRECTLY APPORTIONED

If the store under consideration is a one-department or unit concern, there is no problem of apportionment of indirect expense, and the items of expenditure may be grouped easily in accordance with the symbol to get any totals desired. If you want to know, for instance, your total expenditures for freight, express and cartage, all you have to do is to total all the AT items. If you want to segregate the expense of delivery companies, freight, messengers, and parcels post, simply redivide into ATD, ATF, ATM, and ATP, respectively. If, on the other hand, you want to get the total cost of handling goods and customers, that is, the auxiliary expenses, total all the A's; or if you want your total administrative expenses, take the sum of all the B's. The entire indirect cost of your alterations and repairs is simply the total of the AL items. Your buying expense is the sum of DB for all departments, that is, it will include DBA, DBB, DBC, DBF, DBN, DBR, DBS, DBT, and DBX (if the loss on sales is charged against buying). Similarly, all your advertising expense is easily closed into a control account AA, composed of all those items the symbol for which includes AA as its first two letters.

All this means that every expense should have a voucher, to which the proper symbol is affixed; but if this is done, the resultant ease of handling is what makes the system worth while.

If, however, the store in question is organized in two or more departments, it becomes highly desirable to apportion the indirect expense in some fair way over departments. Such an apportionment properly made often shows wide variations in the profit from different departments, and may even reverse the current opinion of the management as to their relative money-making capacity.

This becomes a highly important practical question as it is nothing unusual to find the profits of one department eaten up by the losses of another. This may sometimes be tolerated as a permanent condition where the maintenance of the loss-producing department is desired as an advertising feature or as a convenience to customers; but even in that case the management should be in a position to know what this advertising and convenience are costing it.

The problem of apportioning indirect expenses over departments is not difficult if sufficient thought is given it in advance, and the method of apportionment indicated in the symbol for the expense. This is another story, however, and meat for another article, and will be discussed fully in the February issue.

ARTICLE III

MAKING EACH DEPARTMENT PAY ITS SHARE

SPEAKING on Keeping Up With Rising Costs before groups of business men, SYSTEM'S lecturer finds that only the most successful merchants have realized the importance of prorating expenses against the departments of the business. Occasionally it is good policy to let one department, such as a restaurant, run at a loss, but no merchandising venture is worth while unless it pays, and only a careful departmentizing of accounts will show which departments are profitable and which run at a loss. Mr. Thompson has shown how the principles of the Taylor system of scientific management have been applied. In this article he points out in detail just how to go about classifying and tabulating expenses under different department heads. The first and last lesson of experience is departmentize your business. When each department pays the business will pay

BY C. BERTRAND THOMPSON *Illustrated with* PHOTOGRAPHIC CHARTS

IT is highly important, as last month's article pointed out, that a department store should know what share of its indirect expenses should be charged against each department. In the absence of such information it is not at all unusual to find a department, supposed to be making a profit, actually running at a loss. In fact, instances have been known where the manager would relieve a weak department of any proper share of expense in order to have that department show a profit, with the explanation that he wasn't going to have a department that didn't show a profit. That is the policy of our old friend, the ostrich.

The modern policy is to find out exactly what each department really costs, not only in the amount of merchandise handled through it, but in supervision, accounting, floor-walking, elevator service, general advertising, and the other innumerable features which go to make up the entire expense of a store but which cannot be charged directly against a department. This is the problem of apportionment – to take all those costs which are incurred by the store as a whole and distribute them over the store components as justly as possible.

Some of the more progressive stores have already accepted the principle of the apportionment of expenses over departments; but as a rule their methods of apportionment are, to say the least, crude. It is quite usual to find all the expenses apportioned by the amount of sales. That this is not at all accurate should be evident on brief consideration.

A department selling notions, for instance, may have three times the number of employees, making its cost of supervision greater, and twenty times as much clerical work as the rug and carpet department or the musical instrument department, while its total volume of sales may be less. In this case the rug department would be charged with considerably more than its proper share of the clerical expense and supervision.

On the other hand, the rug and carpet department may occupy three times the space of a jewelry department doing as much business. If, as has happened, rent is distributed on the basis of total volume of sales, the jewelry department will be paying a large part of the rent which the rug department ought to be charged with. The condition is just as bad when indirect expenses are apportioned entirely on the basis of floor space occupied. When this is done, the rug department bears part of the burden which ought to be carried by those departments occupying a small floor space.

There is, in fact, *no one method of apportionment which is either logical or even approximately accurate.* If accuracy is essential – and as competition becomes keener, reasonable accuracy becomes indispensable – the apportionment of indirect expenses should be on the basis of the actual facts; and on this basis there will be at least ten or fifteen different methods of apportionment for different items of expense.

There are certain items of expense for which it is easy to find the proper method of distribution. Take the cash system, for example, consisting of a number of stations of carriers, a group of cash girls, and the necessary printed forms. The expenses involved are wages, repairs and maintenance, small equipment, power, rent (unless the system is owned by the concern), and incidental supplies. According to the cost classification illustrated in the last preceding article in this series (which appeared in the January issue of SYSTEM) this will be symbolized as follows:

AC CASH SYSTEM

*ACA	Wages and salaries
ACC	Repairs and maintenance
ACE	Equipment
ACP	Power
ACR	Rent
ACS	Supplies

When these cash systems are rented, it is at a charge of so much per station. It is fairly obvious, therefore, that the rent should be distributed over departments in proportion to the number of stations in departments. It is clear also that the cost of repairs and maintenance, equipment, supplies, and power is proportionate to the number of stations and should, therefore, be distributed in the same way. On the other hand, wages of girls in the central station are not necessarily proportionate to the number of stations in departments, but rather to the number of sales in departments, and should therefore be distributed on the basis of the number of sales slips. In any case these items are in no way proportional to the total volume of sales or the amount of floor space occupied.

That part of the work of the accounting department which does not deal with purchasing or stock-handling of merchandise, is concerned in the main with daily sales, credits, and monthly bills. The expense of those clerks dealing with sales and credits should most reasonably be distributed over departments in proportion to the number of sales slips as representing most accurately the number of sales, while that of the billing clerks should of course be distributed in proportion to the number of bills entered.

There are facilities provided by a store, such as the information bureau, post office, and waiting-room, the expense of which should be apportioned according to the number of people using them. In other words, they should be distributed over the departments in proportion to the number of people making purchases in the department; and this is evidenced by the number of sales slips. The benefit that the firm derives from an educational department if it maintains one, is also proportional to the number of sales made; and this expense should therefore be apportioned on the basis of sales slips.

Take such an item as telephone and telegraph expense. When this is incurred in connection with buying for a department, obviously it should be charged directly against the department buying. There are many telephone and telegraph charges, however, which are not incurred directly by a department but should in some way be distributed. Evidently there is no connection between the telephone calls and the volume of business or the floor space occupied by departments. An easy and sufficiently accurate method is to distribute them in propor-

*In practice, in making up a classification, it is desirable invariably to put down all the letters of the alphabet, omitting "I" and "O." Letters not used are omitted here and elsewhere in this article from considerations of space.

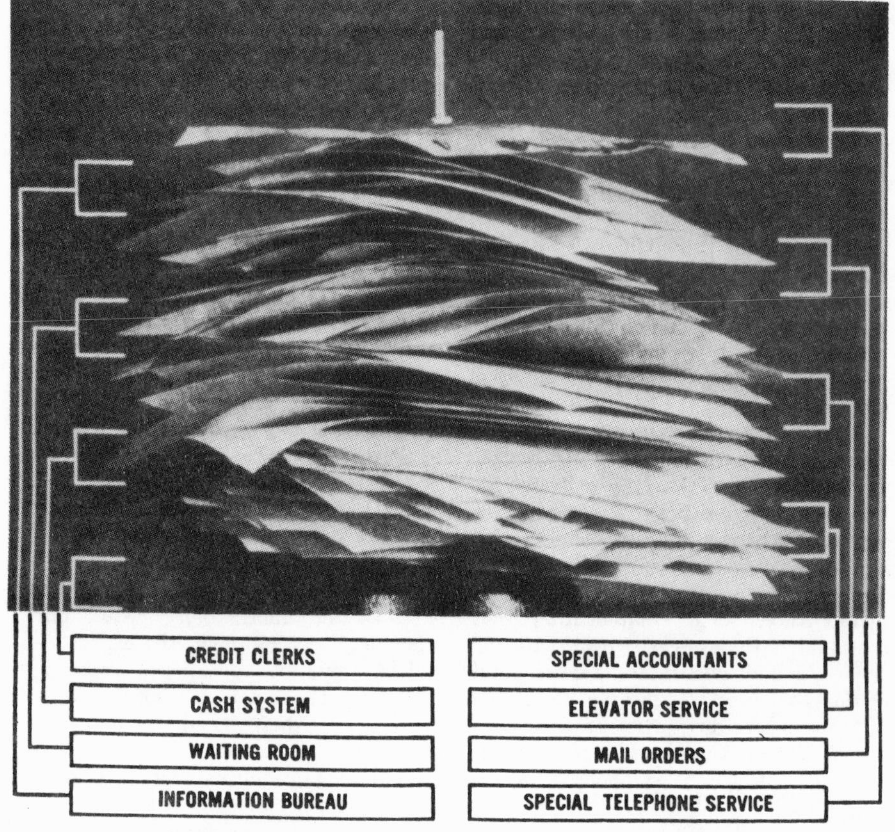

THE EIGHT EXPENSE ITEMS LISTED ARE MOST FAIRLY APPORTIONED BY PRORATING THE TOTAL OF EACH ON THE BASIS OF THE NUMBER OF SALES MADE IN THAT DEPARTMENT

tion to the average number of calls directly charged against departments.

There are many kinds of expense which should be distributed on the basis of the number of square feet occupied by departments. Rent, for instance, is clearly on this basis. Heat, light, ventilation and power, not already charged directly to a department, should be apportioned on the same basis. Janitor service also is generally in proportion to square feet of floor space.

On the same basis is the repairs and maintenance of sprinkler system. Where floor-walkers have a round that includes more than one department, their cost should be distributed also on the number of square feet.

There are many other bases of apportionment, each of which has its own particular application. If a stock-room for supplies is maintained, the expense of this stock-room should be distributed in proportion to the value of supplies used by each department. Insurance on stock should be spread over the average stock carried by departments. The cost of window-dressing should be charged in proportion to window space occupied by each department.

Advertising is usually to be charged directly against the department advertised; but in all advertising there is a large element which is general: that is, which advertises the store as a whole and from which each department gets some indeterminate share of benefit. Such items as billboards and contributions to charity fall into this class. General advertising in newspapers should be distributed over departments in proportion to the total advertising space taken by the department during the year. This applies only to such general advertising as appears in newspapers. Other general advertising cannot be distributed in any way proportionately to the benefit derived by a department, for the reason that such proportionate benefit cannot be ascertained. The disposition of this expense will be discussed later in this article.

Delivery expenses, to be accurate, should be distributed in accordance with the number of parcels shipped from each department. The expense of an employment bureau and liability insurance should be charged on the basis of the department payroll; as these obviously vary with the number of persons employed and their wages or salaries.

The elevator expense offers a special problem. It is not exactly fair to distribute it over the entire store in proportion to the number of people using a department, nor on the basis of floor space, for departments on the street floor have no use for the elevator at all, and, therefore, should not be charged with any part of the elevator expense. The best plan seems to be to distribute it in proportion to the number of sales in the basement and second and upper floor departments.

If the concern does a small mail-order business, not sufficient to warrant a sep-

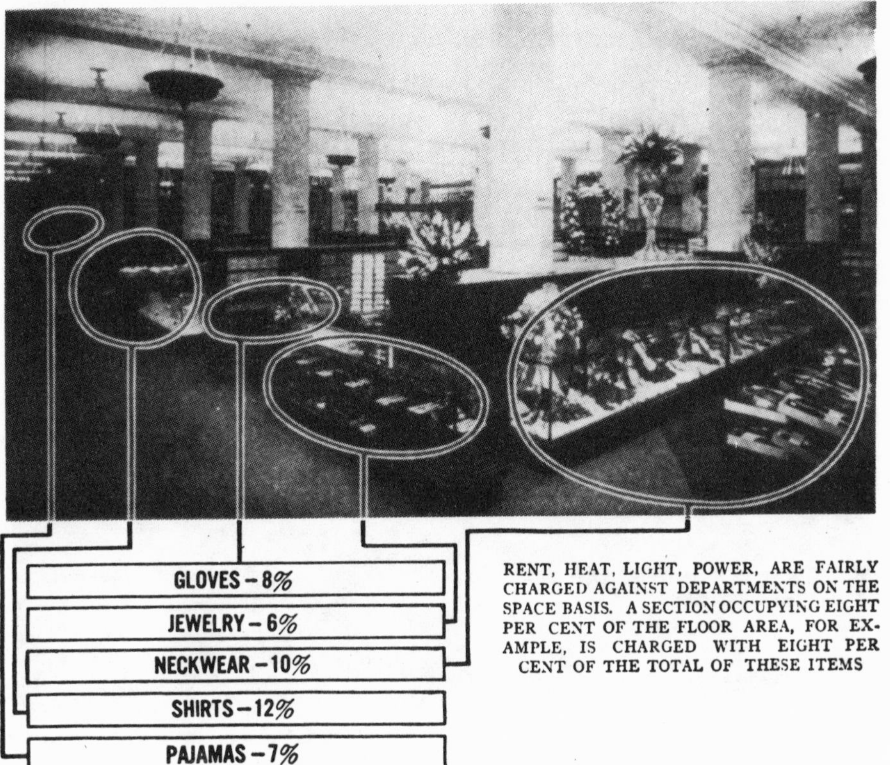

RENT, HEAT, LIGHT, POWER, ARE FAIRLY CHARGED AGAINST DEPARTMENTS ON THE SPACE BASIS. A SECTION OCCUPYING EIGHT PER CENT OF THE FLOOR AREA, FOR EXAMPLE, IS CHARGED WITH EIGHT PER CENT OF THE TOTAL OF THESE ITEMS

arate mail-order department to which the cost may be charged directly, the expense of its mail orders should of course be distributed in proportion to the mail orders filled by departments.

There remain quite a number of expenses which cannot be allocated logically on any of the bases stated. For instance, general advertising not in newspapers, general office expenses, stock-room expense, shipping and receiving department cost, general transportation charges, legal, protective, statistical, "shopping," and system expenses – this means of course all expenses falling in these groups which cannot be charged at once and directly against departments. Something might be said for distributing these in proportion to the total sales of a department but, as the total sales basis is such an easy one to abuse, it is preferable to eliminate it altogether. These general expenses might with at least equal justice be distributed equally to departments and, as they are the only ones that can be so distributed with any logic whatever, that method is to be preferred as the danger of abuse is less.

We thus have fourteen bases of distribution of expenses:

1. Number of square feet.
2. Advertising space taken by department.
3. Window space occupied.
4. Number of sales slips.
5. Number of bills entered for departments.
6. Number of sales in basement, second and upper floors.
7. Number of parcels delivered.
8. Number of mail orders filled by departments.
9. Average stock.
10. Number of carrier stations.
11. Value of supplies used by department.
12. Average number of calls for departments.
13. Payroll.
14. Equally to departments.

THE RUG DEPARTMENT IN THE B. F. ALTMAN STORE IN NEW YORK, SHOWING THE IMMENSE AMOUNT OF FLOOR SPACE REQUIRED FOR ADEQUATE DISPLAY

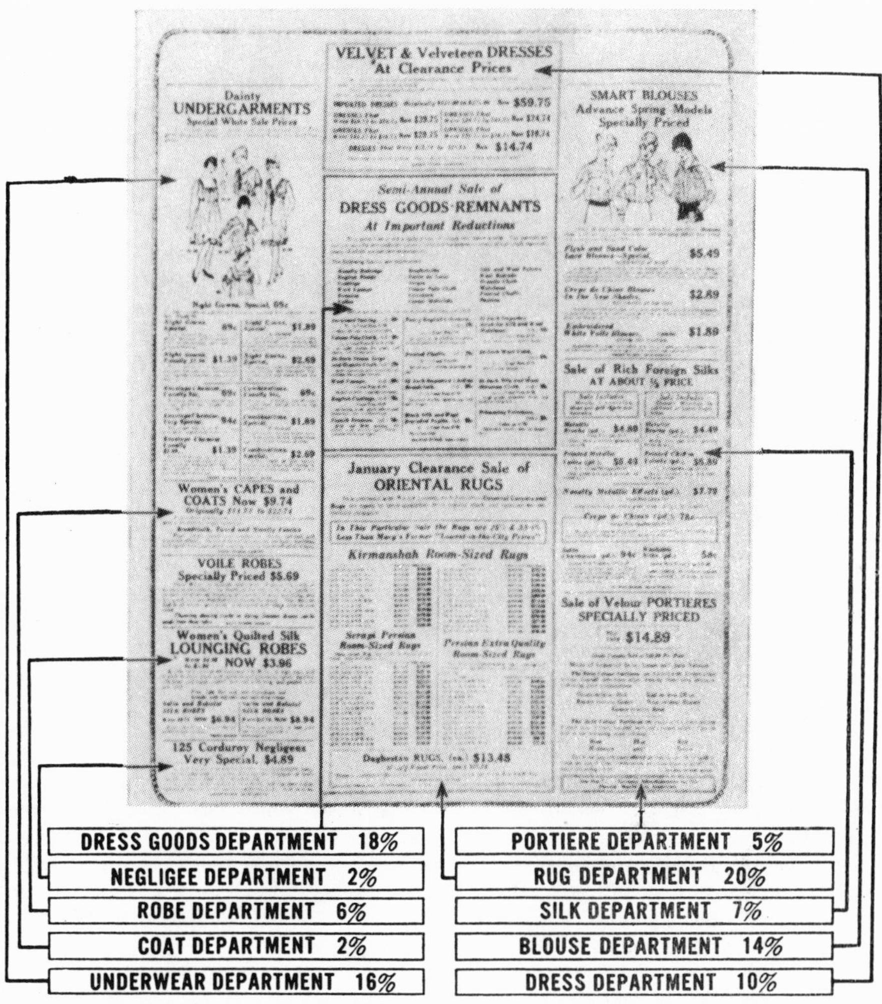

THE TOTAL EXPENDITURE FOR GENERAL ADVERTISING IN NEWSPAPERS IS CHARGED AGAINST DEPARTMENTS IN PROPORTION TO THE AMOUNT OF SPACE TAKEN BY THE DEPARTMENT

The administration of this system is not so difficult as might appear on the surface, if it is thoroughly and carefully worked out in advance. Distribution by departments calls of course for a definite determination of the number of departments involved. Distribution by number of sales slips involves totaling the number of sales slips from each department for each week, if the distribution is made weekly.

Apportionment of expenses by number of square feet means measuring the area of each department and getting its proportion to the total "productive" area of the store (meaning, by "productive," space actually used by selling departments*).

*Productive and unproductive in this sense are accounting terms and do not mean at all that space used for a stockroom, for example, is unproductive, but merely that this expense cannot be charged directly against a department but must be distributed on some basis over all departments.

Bookkeepers' expense is most fairly determined according to the number of bills entered for the departments, and requires a weekly total of this number; similarly with distribution by number of mail orders and telephone calls.

Apportionment of expense by value of supplies used requires that supplies issued to the department shall be issued on requisition, with the values noted on the requisitions and totaled at the end of the week. Advertising space and window space occupied must be measured. Payroll and average stock are already available for the management. The number of stations of the carrier system is easily ascertained. The number of parcels delivered must be kept track of by departments.

With these data once secured, any good clerk with the aid of a calculating machine or a slide rule can make the necessary distribution quickly, if she knows how each item is to be distributed. That is taken care of very simply by numbering the methods of distribution, as in the list above, and inserting the number in the cost symbol on vouchers, the symbol being determined as described in the previous article.

Reference to the preceding article will show how the symbols for expense classification are developed, using the letters of the alphabet. Briefly, a major classification sheet is first laid out in which the letters of the alphabet in order symbolize the various broad divisions of the business. In this base sheet A stands for auxiliary expense, B for administrative expense and so on. Each one of these symbols is then taken and a subdivision of items made for each letter. Listed under administrative expense the separate sheet reads BA, accounting department, BE, educational department and so on.

Now in making up the exact symbols for the subdivision in turn of these items, the plan is to leave a space between the base letters B and A for examples and to develop the detail symbols which the clerk is to use in making vouchers.

For this purpose the cost symbols for specific items should be written with a space between the first and second letters, this space being filled in with the number of the distribution method explained in this article. The cost symbols for the accounting department will be as follows:

B-A Accounting Department

B-AA Salaries and wages
B4AC Repairs and maintenance
B4AE Equipment
B4AR Reclamation of errors
B4AS Supplies and stationery

Salaries and wages distributed differently must have a different base sheet:

B-AA Salaries and Wages

B4AAA Auditors
B5AAB Bookkeepers
B4AAC Cashiers

If every payroll voucher in the accounting department has the symbol stamped on it, every one marked "B4AA" will be distributed on the basis of the number of sales slips; while "B5AAB" will be on the basis of the number of entered. The application of this to the rest of the system can be easily made.

It would be vain to pretend that this system of apportionment is a family necessity. It is not intended for the small, single-line store. It is meant only for department stores or for other stores organized departmentally. For them some system of apportionment is a necessity, and the justification of this particular one is that it comes considerably closer to accuracy than any of the methods now in common use in department stores. It is for them a necessity because, without it, they cannot know accurately the percentage of profit or loss they are making on departments; without it they have no accurate guide to changes in buying, selling and advertising policy; without it they cannot make an intelligent mark-up, nor can they know accurately the cost of mark-down; and it is daily becoming more and more true that, without such a system, they cannot meet permanently the increasing competition of ambitious newcomers in retailing. With such a system intelligently administered they can do all these things.

RECORDS THAT HELP YOU TO MERCHANDISE

THAT business principles are interchangeable is proved by the existence of SYSTEM. The series, of which this article is the fourth, again proves the rule. Scientific management has been developed primarily in factories. Mr. Thompson transferred his knowledge of how it worked there to the problems of a good-sized Massachusetts department store. Yet, as this final article shows, not only are general principles transferable, but certain of the detail methods can be transferred bodily. Perhaps after all the greatest difficulty in any business is to assume that the unfamiliar method can be an improvement

BY C. BERTRAND THOMPSON

Illustrated with a CHART

A SCIENTIFICALLY managed factory operates on the basis of definite and accurate knowledge of every detail necessary to the successful prosecution of its business. It makes its product out of raw materials. It knows what raw materials it has ordered, from whom, and when they are to be delivered; it knows the quantity on hand in its storerooms and its cost. It knows how much its current manufacturing orders call for and, therefore, how much of the quantity on hand or on order is reserved for specific orders. It has determined on the basis of current and prospective use just how low it can allow its stock to fall without interfering with production, and how high it can allow it to go without tying up too much capital; and it provides for automatically ordering within these limits.

The factory is so careful about its stores system because the productive process originates there. The product cannot be made or even started in the works unless the raw materials are on hand. The scientifically managed factory is equally careful of the material after it has started on its course. In the first place it charts that course in advance; then it sees that material is guided through it without deviation; and it keeps track all the time of the location of the partly finished product on its course, until it arrives finally in the stock-room and is shipped to the customer. This constant keeping tabs on the material is not an easy thing to do and has had to justify itself by its results. What it accomplishes is this: first, standardization of materials by elimination of those not necessary or not best adapted; second, reduction of the amount of capital tied up in raw materials; third, a guarantee that raw materials are on hand when needed; fourth, accurate knowledge of the progress of the product through the shop, enabling reasonable promise dates to be given; fifth, control of the finished stock, making prompter shipments possible. This last result, delivery to the customer, is the end and aim of the manufacturing process.

Delivery to the customer is also the end and aim of the retailing process. In order to insure it, the goods to be delivered must have been ordered, received, transferred to the shelves, and finally delivered. They must be on hand when the customer wants to see them; there must not be so much stock that capital is unnecessarily tied up. The chief and practically the only difference between the requirements for the proper accounting of materials in a factory and in a store lies in the fact that the interval between the receipt of raw materials and the delivery of the product in the factory is longer and includes manufacturing processes, whereas in the store it consists merely in the transfer from the storeroom to the shelves and, in some cases, even that is lacking. The methods of accounting, therefore, which have been found successful in factories should be even more successful and simpler in stores; and this article describes an application of a factory system to merchandising.

Every properly-managed store gets frequent reports of the total sales of merchandise each day. These reports are usually in the form of totals for departments in a department store or for entire lines of goods in other stores, such as men's shoes, women's shoes, or cloaks, dresses, and piece goods. The report usually shows also the value of goods unsold and such incidentals as discounts, returns, and repairs and alterations. On the basis of these detailed reports it is possible for the manager to check up the condition of store or department and to keep in constant touch with its needs. If the department is doing well, no action is necessary; if it is not keeping up to the standard set, the buyer is notified and the necessary steps are taken. These daily records extended over a period of years are sometimes charted by weeks or months, or even daily, and the resultant graphs are used to predict the probable demand.

Such information when secured for the store or the department as a whole has some value, but its usefulness is slight compared with that to be derived from similar information by lines or classes of goods. The most up-to-date stores are using the latter method, and still further subdivide their information by prices; and the result of this analysis is to show what priced goods sell best. Some curious information has been derived by this means. It has been shown pretty conclusively, for instance, that a glove will sell for $1.25 more quickly than if it is marked $1.15; and that a $2.00 glove sells better than one at $1.75, although the quality is the same or inferior.

The greatly increased value of the result when the analysis is by lines and prices raises the presumption that a still more minute analysis will be even more worth while.

No up-to-date factory would follow the lax methods of the average retail store in the handling of its stock. The reports of a factory on raw materials and stock on hand are totaled only when an inventory is wanted. Each article carried has its own stock ledger or balance sheet, and the management may know at any moment precisely the quantity and value of each item in stores, in process, or in stock; and with such detailed information before it, it can control its purchases, the routing of its materials, and its investment of capital with the utmost effectiveness.

There is apparently no reason other than custom why retail stores should not follow the same procedure. There should be no more excuse for over-time work or even closing down for stock-taking in a store than in a factory; and the most progressive factories have ceased to interrupt their business for inventory. The value of a perpetual inventory is so well known and so generally acknowledged that no argument should be needed in its support.

And there is a far stronger reason why a store should know exactly and in detail how each item it carries is selling than that a factory should know how its raw materials are going. In general the success of a store depends upon the rapidity of its turn-over, assuming of course that each turn-over is at a profit. Rapid turnover means a comparatively small investment of capital and great elasticity in stock. In stores carrying seasonable goods or goods strongly affected by changes in fashion, frequent turn-over is absolutely necessary to keep the stock up to date and prevent loss through rapid obsolescence.

It usually happens that the advantages of rapid turn-over vary with different items. In the first place, where the profit is large, the turn-over need not be so rapid as in those cases where the margin is small. In the second place, in any given line of goods, such as dress goods, for example, certain materials are staple and the fashion in them does not change

HOW THE MERCHANDISE MANAGER OF A DEPARTMENT

Description ______________________

Kind of unit ______ Mark-up ____

BALANCE OF MERCHANDISE

INSTRUCTIONS FOR POSTING
A – When Merchandise is Ordered, Add Quantity to Column 1.
B – When Merchandise Arrives, Subtract the Quantity Received from Column 1 and Add to Column 2.
C – If Quantity Received is a Partial Shipment, Bring Down Balance Due on Same Purchase Order in Column 2.

1 – MERCHANDISE ORDERED but not yet received								2 – MERCHANDISE RECEIVED IN STOCK-ROOM							
DATE ORDERED	DATE RECEIVED	PURCHASE ORDER NO.	QUANTITY	BILLED COST	DISCOUNT	NET COST		DATE RECEIVED	QUANTITY RECEIVED	PURCHASE ORDER NO.	DELIVERY CHARGES	TOTAL COST	COST PER UNIT	QUANTITY DUE ON ORDER	

COLUMN 1 shows the materials ordered but not yet received. It is made up from a copy of the purchase order which comes from the buyer after being O.K'd or confirmed by the proper authority, and shows the date ordered, date received, purchase order number, quantity ordered, billed cost, discount, and net cost. It is not necessary to enter on this sheet the name of the source of supply. If for any reason it is wanted, it can easily be found by reference to the copy of the purchase order filed numerically. If it is desirable to know whether the order is placed with a jobber or a manufacturer, a J or an M may be entered after the order number.

COLUMN 2 shows the quantity and total cost of the item received in the stock-room (which in the case of a small store is the store itself). Its sub-columns have date received, quantity, purchase order number, delivery charges, total cost (which is the net cost plus the delivery charges), by simple division the cost per unit, and the quantity still due upon order in case of partial shipment.

By comparing columns 1 and 2, it is easy to see which orders are delayed in shipment and need tickling, and the balance still to be delivered. Column 2 shows the cost per unit, which is the basis of the mark-up.

frequently; while others are in today and out tomorrow. Here a quick turn-over is essential. Obviously a report which totals results from all these types of merchandise gives a mere average composite picture which is true neither of the staples nor the novelties, nor of the big profit and small profit items.

In this matter, as so frequently in business, ultimate success depends upon attention to detail, which means again analysis and classification.

Frequently the steps necessary to be taken to secure such detailed analysis are not difficult. The totals now given the manager presuppose items from which

STORE CAN CONTROL DAY BY DAY HIS STOCK ON HAND

When Quantity on Hand in Stock-room falls to ____________
Issue Order for ____________
When Quantity on Hand on Floor falls to ____________
Issue Requisition for ____________
Location in Stock-room ____________
Location on Floor ____________

Symbol

D — When Merchandise is Issued to Department, Strike Balance and Enter in Column 3.
E — When Merchandise is Receipted for by Department, Enter in Column 4.
F — Daily Totals of Merchandise Sold Should be Entered in Column 4, and Balance Left on Hand in Department Entered
NOTE: In All Cases Set Down at Once Balance on Hand in Each Column Affected

3 – MERCHANDISE ON HAND IN STOCK-ROOM							4 – MERCHANDISE ON FLOOR										
DATE ISSUED TO DEPT	QUANTITY ISSUED	ISSUED FOR REQ. NO.	PRICE PER UNIT	TOTAL PRICE	BALANCE ON HAND		DATE RECEIVED	QUANTITY RECEIVED	REQUISITION NO.	DATE SOLD	QUANTITY SOLD NET	PRICE	QUANTITY SOLD AT DISCOUNT	DISCOUNT	NET PRICE	TOTAL SALES	QUANTITY ON HAND

COLUMN 3 is intended to show mainly the merchandise on hand in the stock-room and its price when the goods are not placed directly on the shelves. Deduct the quantity issued to the department or to the shelves from the total quantity received in column 2 and enter the balance in the column, "Balance on hand," in column 3. Column 3 provides for the date of issue from the stock department to the shelves, the quantity issued, the requisition number on which the issue is made, the price per unit (which is the total cost from column 2 plus the mark-up), the total price of the issue, the department, and the balance on hand secured as just described.

COLUMN 4 is the account of actual sales in the department. It shows first, the date received from the stock-room, the quantity, requisition number; and these three sub-columns should check with similar sub-columns in column 3. Column 4 shows daily the quantity sold net, the total price of this quantity, the quantity sold at a discount, the rate of discount, and the total net price of such discount sales, together with the total of all sales. Finally, by deducting the sum of the quantity sold net and the quantity sold at a discount from the total quantity received, column 4 shows the quantity still on hand in the department.

the totals are built up. In order to make the system complete, all that is necessary is that each of these items shall be carried on a merchandise ledger or balance sheet of its own. This does not involve much more clerical work than is now already undertaken. When this is done, the balances shown for each item can be easily combined by classes in such groups as are similar from any point of view in which the management is interested: for instance, by price ranges, by rate of depreciation, as staples, novelties, and so on. With such detailed reports before them, the manager and the buyer cannot help but be more intelligently guided in their decisions. In addition such an accounting provides a perpetual inventory of the store.

The detail of the method to be followed is illustrated in the forms reproduced herewith. These forms may be combined on one sheet and kept by merchandise clerks in the accounting department; this takes away practically all clerical work from stockkeepers, salespeople, and buyers, and concentrates it in the clerical department, where it belongs. Experience has shown this to be the best method in factories where the system is working most successfully. If for any reason, however, this arrangement is not desirable, the forms may be separated and columns 1 and 4 kept in the accounting department and columns 2 and 3 in the stock-room. The description of their use will assume that they are kept together in the accounting department, and will be based on the practice of a department store. Modifications to meet other conditions may readily be made.

Each sheet is the account for each item carried in stock: for example, boy's two-piece suit, blue, No. 531 – the sheet may be subdivided by ruling clear across it horizontally to provide a section for each size.

The items in column 1 are made up from a copy of the purchase order, those in column 2 from the stockkeeper's report of quantity received and the vouchers for delivery charges, column 3 is derived from the department requisitions, and column 4 from the daily sales slips. The system is thus very simple and easy to administer. In case more checks are desired on the quantity and quality of goods received, further detail may be developed for the purpose. The extent to which this is done will depend upon the size and other conditions of each individual concern.

It is the business of the stockkeeper to call the attention of the buyer whenever the balance on hand falls to a predetermined minimum. The buyer will then decide whether to re-order. The minimum limit should be so set that, if it is desired to re-order, there will be enough goods still on hand to meet customers' requirements until the new shipment is received. This depends therefore upon the rapidity with which goods are being sold and upon the probable length of time between order and shipment. To set this minimum limit calls for the exercise of considerable judgment; and in general it should err on the side of too much rather than too little, if it is the policy of the store always to meet its customers' needs.

When the quantity on hand falls to a predetermined minimum, the responsible person in the department requisitions the stock-room for more goods. This requisition must of course go first through the balance clerk in the accounting department to see that the goods are in stock, and if they are, to make the necessary entries debiting the requisitioning department.

At the head of each balance sheet must be entered the following items of information: a description of the article, the kind of unit, the minimum of merchandise in the stock-room at which point the balance clerk is to notify the buyer, the minimum of merchandise in the department or on the shelves at which point the department head is to notify the stockkeeper, and the location of the item in the stock-room and on the floor. The minimum on hand in the department at which point a further requisition is to be issued is kept by the balance clerk as a check on the department head. The latter must of course be supplied also with the same minimum.

It is advisable to print at the head of the sheet a summary of the instructions for posting, as it will be found in practice that it takes balance clerks of average intelligence a month or more to get the balances in shape and keep them there. It must also be remembered that no balance sheet can remain accurate very long without frequent checking, at first by actual count of the quantities on hand in the stock-room and in the department. For awhile it will be advisable to check every sheet as often as possible, even if this necessitates double the force of clerks for a month or two. After that the sheets may be divided into groups in such quantities that the entire stock will be covered say once in three months, by checking one group each day.

For convenience of filing, brevity in writing, and definite identification of each item (which in practice often goes by a variety of names), it is usually desirable to symbolize each item. The method of mnemonic symbolization, which I believe to be the best for general purposes, was described fully in a former article on "Listing Stock to Index Wastes" in the March, 1913, number of SYSTEM. It may be interesting to illustrate how this works out in practice. "M" is the first letter in the symbol for "Merchandise." In a department store this would be followed by a "D" for department, with the number of the department between the "M" and the "D." It is advisable to number departments where there are many of them rather than attempt to give them mnemonic symbols. In a one-line store the hyphen and the "D" are omitted and the symbol for the class of articles to be symbolized falls immediately after the "M" unless there are several items of the same article but with different dimensions, in which case the distinguishing dimensions are included after the "M."

Suppose we start with our original cost base sheet (see SYSTEM, December, 1914).

A Auxiliary expense	M (Merchandise)
B Adminis. expense	N
C	P
D Depart. expense	R
E	S (Stores and supplies)
F	T
G	U
H	V
J	W
K	X
L	

Y Fixtures, machinery and equipment, except that which is written off when purchased.
Z Land and buildings.

Suppose the kitchen ware department is No. 2. The base sheet for it will be somewhat as follows:

*M2DA	Aluminum
M2DC	Chinaware
M2DD	Seeds, bulbs, shrubbery
M2DE	Earthenware
M2DF	Fibrous ware
M2DG	Glassware
M2DH	Hardware
M2DK	Crockery
M2DL	Lighting fixtures
M2DM	Enamel and agate ware
M2DN	Nickel ware
M2DP	Copper ware
M2DR	Rubber goods
M2DS	Steel and iron ware
M2DT	Tinware
M2DV	Stoves
M2DW	Wooden ware
M2DX	Miscellaneous, not elsewhere classified

The base sheet for chinaware will be this:

M2D-CA Plates	M2D-CP Pitchers
M2D-CB Bowls	M2D-CS Saucers
M2D-CC Cups	M2D-CT Platters
M2D-CD Sauce dishes	

Plates, bowls, and so on, will have their dimensions inserted where the hyphen appears after the "D."

For a grocery store or grocery department, the following base sheet will usually be found sufficient:

M7DB	Beverages
M7DC	Cereals and cereal products
M7DD	Dairy products, not elsewhere classified
M7DE	Extracts, syrups and colorings
M7DG	Gelatine, baking powder, and other cooking compounds, not elsewhere classified
M7DH	Herbs, seasonings, condiments, and spices, not elsewhere classified
M7DM	Meats and fish, not perishable
M7DP	Pickles, olives, olive oil
M7DS	Soaps, cleansers, polishers
M7DU	Fruits and nuts, not perishable
M7DV	Vegetables, not perishable
M7DX	Miscellaneous

If this department carries fresh vegetables, they might be put under M7DF; fresh meats under M7DT.

The following subdivisions will illustrate the subject further:

M7DBD	Dry beverages
M7DBW	Wet, except milk and cream (for which see dairy products)

Dry beverages will be further subdivided, as for example:

*In practice in making up a classification, it is desirable invariably to put down all the letters of the alphabet, omitting "I" and "O." Letters not used are omitted here and elsewhere in this article from considerations of space.

M7DBDB	Bouillon cubes	M7DBDK	Cocoa
M7DBDC	Coffee	M7DBDM	Malted milk
M7DBDD	Drugs	M7DBDT	Tea
M7DBDH	Chocolate		

And the different brands of cocoa, for instance, may be designated thus:

M7DBD1K Baker's cocoa
M7DBD2K Lowney's cocoa
M7DBD3K Van Houten's cocoa
M7DBD4K Trinity cocoa
M7DBD5K Runkel's cocoa

Where there are different sizes or weights for the same article, they may be indicated as follows:

M7D¼B1W Grape juice, 4 oz.
M7D½B1W Grape juice, ½ pt.
M7D 1 B1W Grape juice, 1 pt.
M7D 2 B1W Grape juice, 1 qt.

Department No. 8, handling supplies and stationery, would have its goods classified in this way:

M8DA Blank cards
M8DB Blotting papers
M8DC Chairs
M8DD Desks
M8DE Erasers
M8DF Files and filing cabinets
M8DH Card holders
M8DK Inks
M8DN Blank books
M8DP Pens, penholders, and pencils
M8DR Ribbons, typewriter, adding machine
M8DS Paste
M8DT Tables
M8DU Rubber bands
M8DW Writing paper, unprinted

It may be interesting to set out in detail the classification of stock for a shoe department, which for convenience we will call Department 10. The base sheet will be:

M10D-A	Athletic	M10D-W	Women's
M10D-M	Men's	M10D-S	Special
M10D-N	Infants'		

M10D-M, Men's Shoes, is subdivided:

M10D-M-H High M10D-M-L Low

Further subdividing Men's High Shoes, we have the following:

M10D-M-HC	Cloth	M10D-M-HR	Rubber
M10D-M-HF	Calf	M10D-M-HS	Substitutes
M10D-M-HK	Kid		
M10D-M-HP	Patent	M10D-M-HV	Vici

Men's High Calf Shoes would be subdivided as follows:

M10D-M-HFB Blucher
M10D-M-HFC Congress
M10D-M-HFS Straight lace
M10D-M-HFT Button

Each shoe is built on a last peculiar to itself and has a size, width, and color. The last number should be filled in where the hyphen appears after the "D"; the size and width after the "M," and the color should come last. If the last number includes a letter, the combination should be put entirely in parenthesis, in order not to confuse the letter with the rest of the symbol, as should also the size and width. If, for instance, the shoe to be symbolized is a Kelwain, last No. 297, size 9, width B, and light tan, in a men's calf blucher, the symbol would be:

M10D(K297)M(9B)HFB1T

T meaning tan, and 1 light tan; medium tan will be 2T; dark tan 3T, and so on.

Any system of stock handling which is more complex and cumbersome than those now in use would hardly be justified, unless there is a great deal to commend it. Fortunately the system described in this article is far *less* complicated and cumbersome than the usual methods, except in those stores which have no method at all. The number of forms required for its efficient operation is small. The amount of clerical work involved is not as great as is usually found in the ordinary systems. The result, when this system is properly administered, is a complete, accurate and up-to-date account of the precise condition of the stock on hand, from which it is easy to deduce the present and probable future demand for each item carried. When the salesman comes in and you want to know what to reorder, and in what quantities, you can get your answer at once from an inspection of the merchandise sheet for your department or store, without going outside the office for it. When you want to know the total value of all stock on hand all you have to do is to total the values given on these sheets, and there is no necessity for losing three days' trade to take an inventory.

MY PLAN FOR APPLYING "SCIENTIFIC MANAGEMENT" IN AN OFFICE

William H. Leffingwell

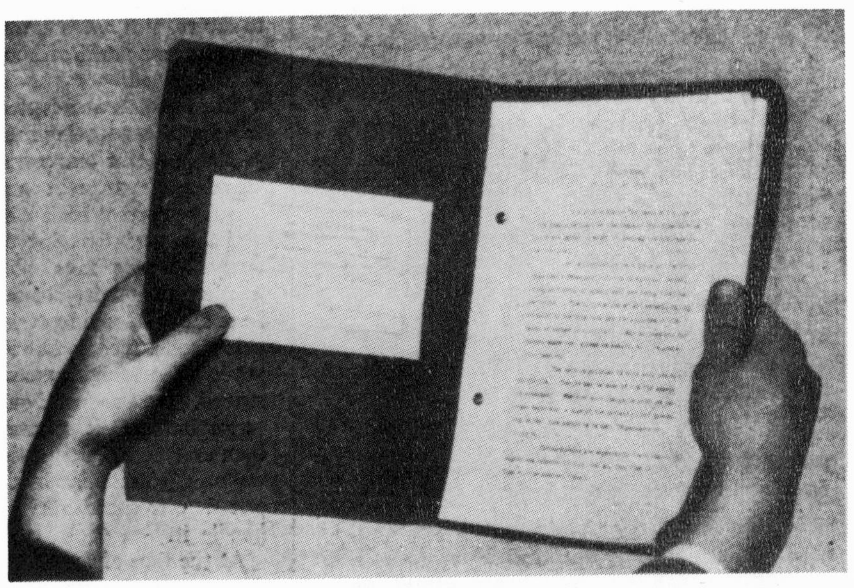

THE POLICY BOOK

In conferences, which all those handling correspondence attended, policies to cover specific problems that came up were formulated and recorded. Only the executive board can change rulings of the policy book

MY PLAN FOR APPLYING "SCIENTIFIC MANAGEMENT" IN AN OFFICE

By W. H. LEFFINGWELL *Illustrated with* Forms

FIVE thousand unanswered letters in the house, a thousand more coming in every day, dozens of orders arriving with every mail, each order and letter requiring a technical expert's handling, and only one correspondent in the house trained as a technical expert – that, in a few words, tells the story of the situation we faced a little over a year ago.

This congestion in our correspondence was caused by the success of a new product and the method we used to market it. Before the war we sold entirely to professional people. Their orders ranged between twenty-five and one hundred dollars each – cash down. After the war broke we found it advisable to make a change in our product. This enabled us to sell practically the same article in a cheaper form for five dollars – and we allowed the smaller sum to be paid in instalments.

Orders and letters began pouring in as soon as we advertised this departure. It had been comparatively simple for the correspondence department to handle four $25 cash orders; it was quite a different task to dispose of twenty $5 instalment orders.

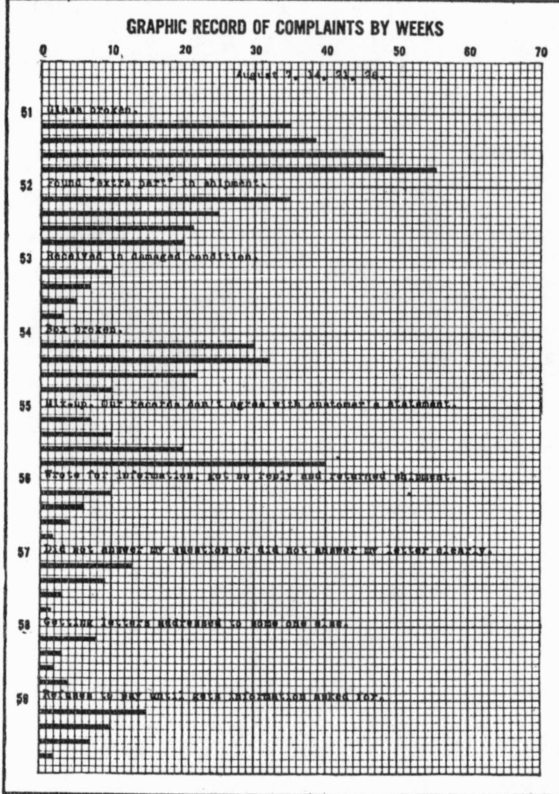

WHY CUSTOMERS COMPLAIN

Each month a graphic summary like this is drawn up. It shows where the most complaints are coming from, and helps the management to correct faults

to arrive, still more correspondence and clerical labor were involved.

The methods we adopted to relieve the resulting congestion and put our correspondence department on a soundly effective basis will probably be interesting to every business man who has letters to write, for we have secured some remarkable results. Today, letters never lie overnight unanswered. The volume of our correspondence is greater than ever, but no longer do we need to employ high-priced correspondents to handle it.

At the time of the severest congestion, we were hiring assistants so rapidly that not enough room could be found in the office. Many had to sit at upturned packing boxes which served as desks. They were tucked away in every spare corner of the building, on three different floors. They had to be trained hurriedly. Indeed, so rapidly were they hired, that little care could be taken in selecting them.

The clerical labor involved in a five-dollar instalment order was much greater. When we sold for cash the money was deposited in the bank and that ended the transaction, in the majority of cases. But when the five-dollar order was entered and the goods shipped, that was just the beginning and several other parts of the transaction had to be performed.

Only one dollar had been deposited in the bank and, theoretically, another dollar was to come along each month for four months. As each of these dollars arrived, another clerical operation had to be performed; each time one failed

Now the work proceeds in an orderly manner, without rush. It is handled by employees thoroughly trained to the best and quickest way.

The first step was to try hiring trained letter writers. That proved a failure. We discovered no one who appeared able to adapt himself to our quite unusual conditions.

We then called upon the employment department for intelligent clerks. Some of the applicants we accepted had only grammar school educations. Others were high school graduates. None had done similar work.

We instructed these clerks to read the correspondence and sort all letters, for a period of several weeks, into a dozen or so broad classes. We then examined this work thoroughly and prepared a set of form letters and form paragraphs to cover the classes selected. By means of these letters and paragraphs the readers were able to answer whole batches of letters by simply jotting down on each one the numbers of the appropriate form letter or series of paragraphs.

This was the first important step. We had to be sure we were right in every detail, however, and as we went along we held frequent consultations. Every point was thoroughly threshed out as soon as it came up.

In these consultations we often took up questions like these:

"What shall we say to a customer who says so and so?"

"What shall we do if a customer does such and such a thing?"

"What attitude are we going to take when the customer . . . ?"

RECORD OF COMPLAINTS HANDLED BY May Smith Week Beginning 8/24/16

No.	Monday	Tuesday	Wednesday	Thursday	Friday	Saturday	TOTAL
50	𝍸 //	//	///	/	////	/	18
1	𝍸 𝍸	///	𝍸	//	𝍸	//	27
2							
3							
4							
5							
6							
7							
8							
9							
60	/	/	/	/			4
1							
2							
3							
4							
5	𝍸 𝍸 𝍸	𝍸	///	////	𝍸		32
6							
7							
8							
9							
70							
1							
2							
3							
4							
5							
6							
7							
8							
9							
80	//						2
1							
2							
3							
4							
5							
6	///		//			/	6
7							
8							
9							
90							
1							
2							
3							
4							
5							
6							
7							
8							
9							
100							

KEEPING TRACK OF COMPLAINTS

Correspondents have sheets like this in front of them. Whenever they handle a complaint letter, they "tally up" a mark against the number that represents that kind of complaint

Whenever we came to a decision, we recorded it, made it "the policy of the house," and gave it a place in our "policy book." Each correspondent and reader was required to study these policies and to act accordingly.

They learned their lessons thoroughly. In fact, the manager, who relied upon his judgment and memory, was occasionally criticised by correspondents for giving orders contrary to the "policy book's" rulings. If the manager felt that the policy questioned was wrong, he could follow only one course – take up the problem with our executive board. He could not instruct the correspondent to act contrary to the "policy book's" rulings.

These policies were, of course, general in their nature and left room for a certain amount of individual judgment. But they had the effect of harmonizing and unifying all our correspondence.

It will be interesting to tell exactly how we arranged to have the letters read and answered. After passing through the mail opening department, they are delivered to the correspondents – or readers, as we call them – in folders, which contain just twenty-five letters each.

The correspondents read every letter carefully. Two-thirds of the letters, we find, can be answered at once. These are handled whenever possible – and it is possible in ninety per cent of the cases, we find – by either standard form letters or form paragraphs. The paragraph system we use will be described in greater detail later.

When it is necessary to consult records before answering, the reader fills out a printed form, briefly summarizing the contents of the letter. This is so arranged that very little writing by the correspondent is necessary. A sample form is shown below.

Date JUN 28 1916
Received in Index Dept. Date
" " Coll. " "
" " Refund " "
" " Claim " "
To Correspondence Dept. Date
JUN 28 REC'D (Shipping Date)
JUN 29 1916

COLLECTION DEPT.
✓ Customer Claims Paid 2 00 Bal. Due
✓ Card Record Date Shipped 6/27/16
Payments Amount of Sale 5 00
Date 89348 6/19/16 Amount 2 00 Postage
" Amount Paid 2 00
" 10 kg : free C. O. D.
" Balance 3 00
Customer Claims Returned Camera
Camera Returned Charges C. O. D.
Refunded

REFUND DEPARTMENT
Customer Asks for Refund

CLAIM DEPARTMENT
A 92 Did Not Receive Camera (Order No. 47959
Camera on Hand at Exp. or P. O. (Tag No. Express
8 Release Camera ANSWERED (Signed by
I 82 Order Camera RETURNED (Also Give Above Card Record
Did Not Receive Supplies Ordered Date
Ordered
Supplies Shipped Date By
What Kind of Camera Has Customer?

Professional Record Free Premium Record
Give Copy Card Unapplied Cash Record
Copy of Supply Shipment Per MAIL READER

REMARKS

THE "LOOK-UP" SHEET

When it is necessary to have records consulted before a letter can be answered, the correspondent attaches one of these slips to it and sends it to the proper department

The letter is next sent to the proper department for the desired information. This department looks up the information, writes it in on the "remarks" space, and the letter is then returned to the correspondence department for further attention. The reader next marks in the numbers of the suitable paragraphs and the letter goes to the typing department, where it is typewritten.

The very fact that correspondence, at the time the reorganization began, was coming in faster than it could be handled, directed special attention to relieving this congestion with form paragraphs and form letters. Whenever a letter is not covered by existing paragraphs or forms, it is marked "special" and given to a trained correspondent to answer. If he finds that the same question is repeated by ten different persons, even over an extended period, a paragraph is written to cover it.

This paragraph is sent to the advertising department, where it is worked over with as much care as though it were copy for an advertisement to appear in a magazine with a circulation of a million. It is then given a number, a master copy is written with a duplicator ribbon, and sufficient copies are duplicated upon cards so that one can be furnished to each typist and correspondent.

If any question is asked more than ten times in any one day, a form letter answering it is made out.

These form paragraphs and letters are classified and numbered according to subjects. Great care is taken to make each paragraph complete, and to

TYPING LETTERS FROM STANDARD PARAGRAPHS

Ninety per cent of the correspondence discussed by Mr. Leffingwell in this article is answered with standard paragraphs or letters. As a result, typists can largely replace more highly paid stenographers

have it deal with one subject only. All the reasonable variations are carefully considered, and paragraphs written to cover them.

Attention is paid, also, to the different moods expressed by customers. All complaints, for example, are handled in a uniformly courteous manner, no matter how provoking the customer may be.

If, as occasionally happens, a certain paragraph only partially answers the customer, the reader jots down an extra sentence to make it fit exactly. This goes on a slip of paper, and the reader adds instructions directing the typist to include the extra sentence in the proper paragraph.

As it stands today, this system of ours contains over five hundred separate paragraphs and one hundred form letters.

The paragraphs – as stated – are carefully indexed by subjects. The correspondents, however, soon learn the most important ones, so they find it unnecessary to consult the index for each letter. Quite often you will hear our correspondents saying something like this to each other:

"What do you do when a customer says he will not pay his account unless we send him some free supplies?"

"Oh, I give him K16, A24 and K36."

"Is that so? Why don't you give him B18, K 36?"

"Because policy No. 32 says ——," and so on.

When you look up the fine points involved in a conversation like this, you usually find that there is some delicate difference between the paragraphs mentioned. No harm would have resulted, probably, if either course had been taken. But it shows the remarkable fitness of each paragraph, and the intelligence with which they are used.

On one occasion, an executive of the company discovered in the files a letter which pleased him greatly.

"Who wrote this letter?" he asked the head of the department. "It is a gem.

You ought to encourage that dictator, for the letter certainly shows ability."

On investigation, we found that the letter consisted of paragraphs only, written at various times. Even the executive had supposed it was a personally dictated letter.

HOW LETTERS ARE "DICTATED" WITH THE STANDARD PARAGRAPHS

It seems probable that the letters written by this paragraph system are superior to the average, specially dictated, personal letter. The reason for that is simple.

More care has been devoted to writing the paragraphs, and phrasing them in precisely the right way, than could ordinarily be given to the work by a dictator, even under the most advantageous circumstances. Hours, in fact, have been given to some of the form paragraphs, and before being finally adopted, they have often been written and re-written many times.

In "dictating" letters under our paragraph system, high school girls have been able to handle as many as fifty or sixty of them an hour. The greatest amount of time goes to reading the customers' letters. From the average dictator who personally formulates each reply, it is hard to get one hundred and fifty letters a day.

Members of our correspondence department show great interest and enthusiasm. They worked splendidly when letters were coming in faster than they could be answered.

An interesting game was then made of the work, and all took part. A large bulletin was placed on the wall in full view of the whole department. This was ruled off into a large number of squares.

I have already explained that letters are given to the readers in batches of twenty-five in folders. So we wrote in the squares on the bulletin the figure "25" as many times as there were folders of unanswered letters. When a folder was handled and turned in, we canceled one "25."

As rapidly as new letters arrived, more "25s" were placed in the blank spaces. The readers struggled with the stream of letters with energy and determination. They did not seem to consider their task hard work, but rather a sport.

During this strenuous period we held a daily discussion class for the readers. This class dealt with problems coming up in the correspondence. Various methods of handling typical cases were discussed and standardized. New paragraphs were suggested. Misunderstandings were uncovered and corrected. These discussions kept the whole force working harmoniously.

We also hold a weekly class for correspondents. This class meets Tuesday evenings, the company providing supper.

It takes up the general subject of writing. We believe that most progress can be made by not confining these lessons to writing letters for the firm – for then the papers might be judged solely on their relationship to the company's problems – but by making them cover the field of writing in general. We have, for example, considered the short story as a model.

The ideal we aim at is to have the tone of our letters as much as possible like one person talking with another – not stilted. To emphasize this, frequent exercises are given. We act out some incident in the class, have it reported verbatim, and afterwards re-written by the class.

We never permit anything to be written in a letter that would not sound natural and fit if spoken.

WHAT THE EMPLOYEES THINK OF THE NEW METHODS

This class has developed some remarkable talent. One girl, only seventeen years old, showed much ability.

This girl's talent would probably never have been discovered in the ordinary routine of a business office. She was shy and retiring. She came to the company as a typist, and proved a failure at that. We tried her at various other jobs, but she did not make a startling success. Finally, she attended the class of her own accord, and submitted some essays that were quite remarkable. She has become a valuable employee, and has increased her earning power because the opportunity was given her to show what she could accomplish.

It might seem that this plan places the business of the company in the hands of inexperienced clerks. How can the management watch all the details? Of course, it is impossible for any one person to read carefully, in a week, one day's mail. This problem of control has been solved with our complaint record.

A sample of the form we use is shown on page 375. The headings are as follows:

Manufacturing faults;
Technical faults;
Accounting and recording;
Loss of money or goods;
Errors in packing and shipping;
New wants of customers;
Correspondence errors.

Each correspondent has on her desk one of the sheets illustrated, and each type of complaint – as you will notice – has a number. As the letters are read, every complaint that comes to the correspondent's notice is recorded by simply scoring a tally mark, as boys score runs in a baseball game.

At the end of the week, these sheets are gathered, totaled, and a graphic record is given to the general manager. The record for four weeks is shown on each graphic sheet. This enables the busy manager not only to get a digest of the various complaints weekly, but to compare them with previous weeks and grasp the situation at a glance. The record is an effective means of control.

This completes my story of one part of our reorganization. I shall tell further details about the methods we use to promote effective work among our stenographers and typists in coming issues of SYSTEM.

THIS PLAN MORE THAN DOUBLED OUR TYPISTS' OUTPUT

William H. Leffingwell

THIS PLAN MORE THAN DOUBLED OUR TYPISTS' OUTPUT

SECOND ARTICLE

Will the principles of "scientific management" work in an office? Before you answer, read this article – it describes the results secured by one concern which made the experiment

By W. H. LEFFINGWELL

Illustrated with CHARTS

WHEN we began to train our typists, their output was far from satisfactory, although they were apparently industrious enough. From the beginning they had always been treated fairly and no petty restrictions placed upon them. As a consequence, there was little tendency on the part of any of them to "stall." However, in spite of their apparent industry, the output of the department was far less than we believed possible.

After certain alterations, which I shall describe in detail in this article, the average output was just about tripled. This, I am confident, is a result that can be obtained – at least in part – in many concerns where similar methods are used.

We started first of all to improve the physical arrangement of the office. Desks were crowded closely together in rows of four. Each time a typist found it necessary to leave her desk, she disturbed possibly three other workers in the same row. This condition we remedied by placing the desks in rows of two, with an aisle on each side. Thus, when it was necessary for one of the girls to leave her seat, no one was disturbed.

The next step came in assigning the work. Formerly it was placed in large boxes, and each typist helped herself as she required it. This resulted in some girls getting too much and others not enough, while often some would pick "easy" work, to the disadvantage of others.

This condition we remedied by having the department manager assign the work, giving each girl just enough to keep her busy and no more.

Stationery also proved to be a problem calling for attention. There were four kinds of letterheads, ten kinds of envelopes, half a dozen kinds of booklets and other miscellaneous types of stationery. Each typist had a supply of every kind. This material she kept in her desk. Many times a day the drawers were pulled out. It meant a lot of waste motion.

We remedied this condition by having special cabinets or racks made which held not only a small quantity of the necessary stationery, but finished and unfinished work as well. One of these cabinets was placed on each typist's desk within easy reach. A small number of letterheads – enough for an hour or so was kept under the typewriter, thus avoiding the necessity even of extending the hand so short a distance as 18 inches to the cabinet.

Often, in the midst of her work, a typist would discover a shortage of a certain kind of stationery and there was an inevitable delay until her stock was replenished. This we remedied by making it the duty of the inspector to keep the cabinet supplied constantly.

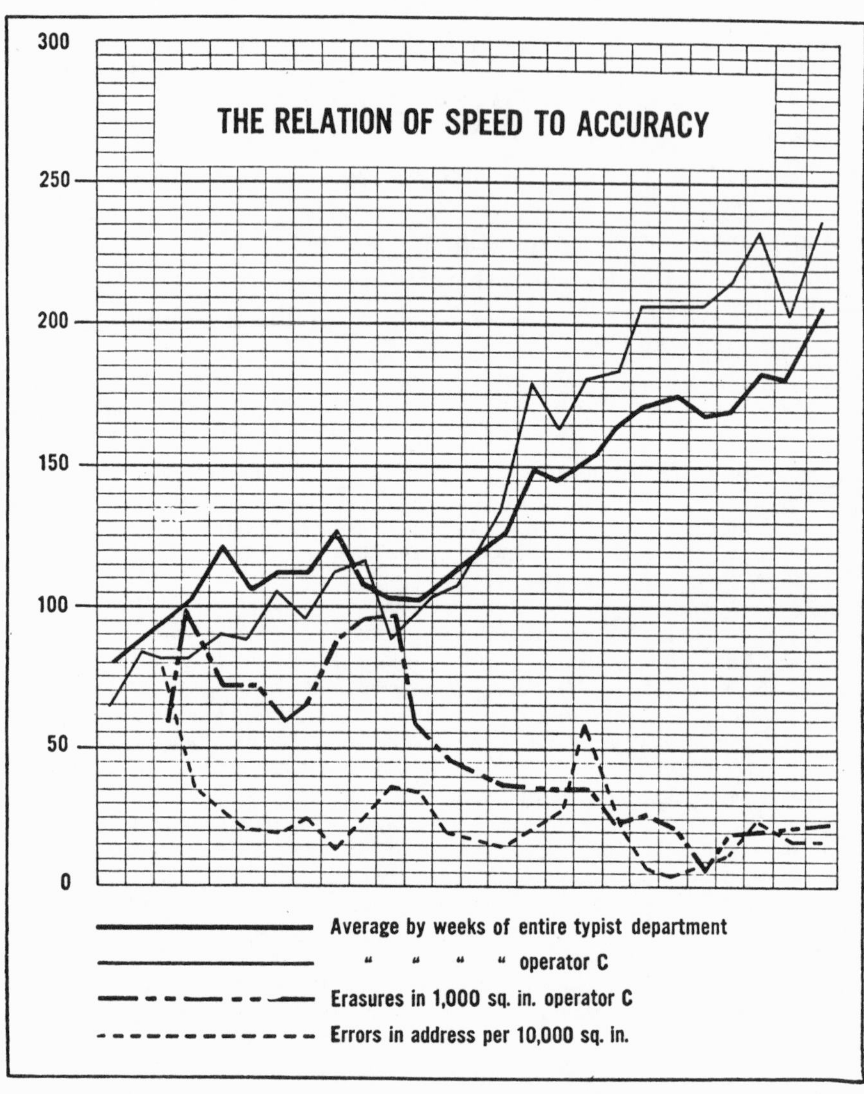

ONE OPERATOR'S RECORD

This is a record by weeks extending over six months of the work of one of the operators under Mr. Leffingwell's direction. She was typing letters. It shows that she began below the average for the department and ended considerably above, in spite of the fact that the department itself progressed from an average of 80 square inches per hour to 200. This operator's average for the first week was 65 inches, and for the last week 237, an increase of nearly 270%.

Note particularly that during the eleventh week, when this operator made a serious effort to increase her efficiency, erasures, which are figured on a percentage basis, dropped. During that week she made 95 erasures for every 1,000 square inches, and she wrote at the rate of 80 square inches per hour. During the final week she made 20 erasures per 1,000 square inches and wrote at the rate of 237 square inches per hour.

The question arises: Did she make fewer errors because she wrote so rapidly, or did she write so rapidly because she made so few errors? Mr. Leffingwell's experience is that rapid work requires concentration, and this results in better work

Formerly, there had been no reliable record of the work done by any one operator. The correspondents had no time to ascertain the quantity of work, and little inclination to criticise the quality. There were about ten different kinds of typewriting done in the department and although it was known that there was such and such a number of girls working in the department, that there was so much work of various kinds done and to be done, it was not known just how much of each kind of work Mary Jones did, nor how long it took her to do it.

WHAT A STUDY OF THE WORK BEING DONE BY THE TYPISTS SHOWED

Certain types of the work were standardized, therefore, and an inspector was detailed to examine, correct and keep careful record of the output of each girl. A daily record of the various types of work done by each girl, and the length of time it took her to do it, was kept.

This record showed some startling results. Those getting the highest salaries were not the most efficient, and some of those who appeared to be the most industrious were not the speediest operators.

We experienced some difficulty at first in getting a correct time record. But we finally solved the problem by using a simple time stamp, and giving each girl a time card for each batch of work of a certain kind that was given her. The work was stamped with the beginning and the finishing time.

We arranged careful inspections for five different kinds of errors, classed according to their importance as follows:

Class 1, Errors in addresses
Class 2, Errors in context
Class 3, Errors in spelling
Class 4, Errors in typing
Class 5, Erasures.

Each operator was shown daily her record of work and errors.

I have sketched briefly a few of the most important details of the plan by which the effectiveness of the department as a whole was improved. The work was not all finished in a day, and was accomplished only by constant study and observation. However, with this preliminary work done we were in a position to improve the individual records of the typists.

As soon as we had reliable comparative records, showing the average work accomplished every hour by each operator, charts of various sorts were posted on the bulletin board to show the progress of each worker. These had an immediate effect on results.

Careful observation for waste motion resulted in a great improvement. For example, we found that erasures constituted one of the most important sources of lost time. And we further discovered that a large portion of the time the reason for erasures was the fact that girls were working in spurts. We urged them to write slowly and deliberately. Whenever this advice was followed, there was an immediate increase in product. The importance of the point was brought to the attention of the girls in about this way:

"Suppose you were running a foot race. You are so anxious to win that you run at the highest possible speed. You run so fast and so recklessly that every twenty feet you trip or stumble. Would you break any speed records? You would not. If you reached the goal at all, you would be so exhausted from spurting, and lose so much time picking yourself up, that you would likely be the last to arrive. Suppose, on the contrary, another ran carefully and deliberately at a steady pace throughout the whole race, without once stumbling – who would win?"

SOME OF THE PLANS THAT HELPED INCREASE THE OUTPUT

Each operator was taught that there was only one right way to put a piece of paper in the machine. We showed her how to do this without waste of time. By time studies we discovered that different operators took for this operation all

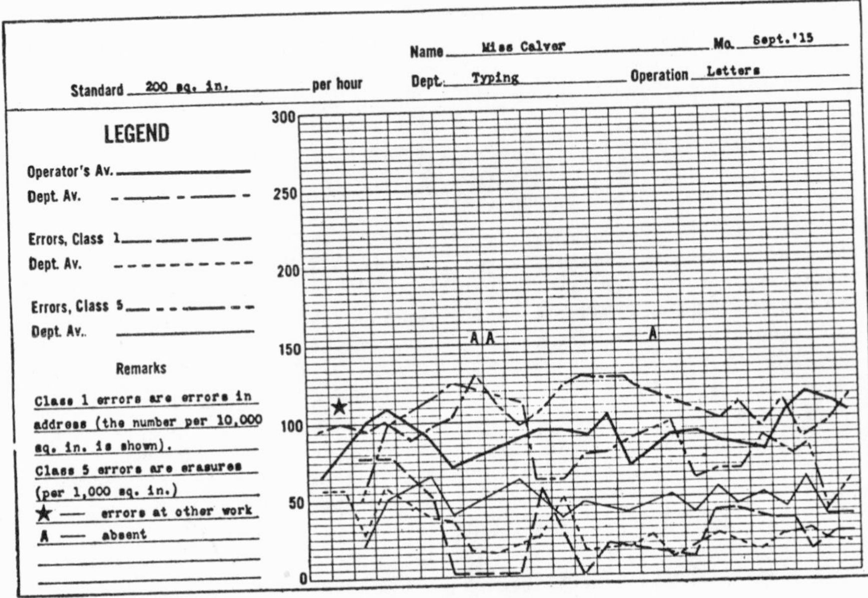

AN OPERATOR'S OUTPUT AT THE START–

A monthly record like this is kept of the output of each typist, showing graphically what her progress has been from day to day. Note how this girl's record for September–shown above–contrasts with her record for January, four months later, as shown in the chart on the opposite page

the way from three hundredths of a minute to one-half minute. If an operator took one-half minute to adjust the letterhead in the machine and did this sixty times a day, that operation alone would require one-half hour, whereas if done in the shortest possible time it ought to occupy not more than .03 x 60 or 1.8 minutes, leaving 28.2 minutes more in which to write letters.

Another reason for inefficiency was improper sitting at the desk. Some girls would sit on the edge of their chairs, tipping at a dangerous angle and twisting their feet around the legs of the chairs. This is not an exaggeration. Many such cases were discovered. We taught them to sit well back in the chairs, with the feet placed squarely on the floor and head and shoulders erect. The correct and incorrect positions are shown on page 466.

One inexperienced operator, we observed, turned her head to read her copy on an average twenty times a minute. We pointed out to her that if she kept up that record for one day, consisting of eight and one-half hours, she would have twisted her neck over ten thousand times. We suggested that she abandon this fatiguing habit and learn to read and remember at least twenty or twenty-five words for each twist of the head. Later, this observation led to the installation of a special copyholding device which altogether obviated the turning of the head.

All chairs and desks were formerly the same height, but, unfortunately, all of the operators were not. So we furnished cushions to those who needed to be elevated.

After eliminating the most obvious faults of the individual operators, we

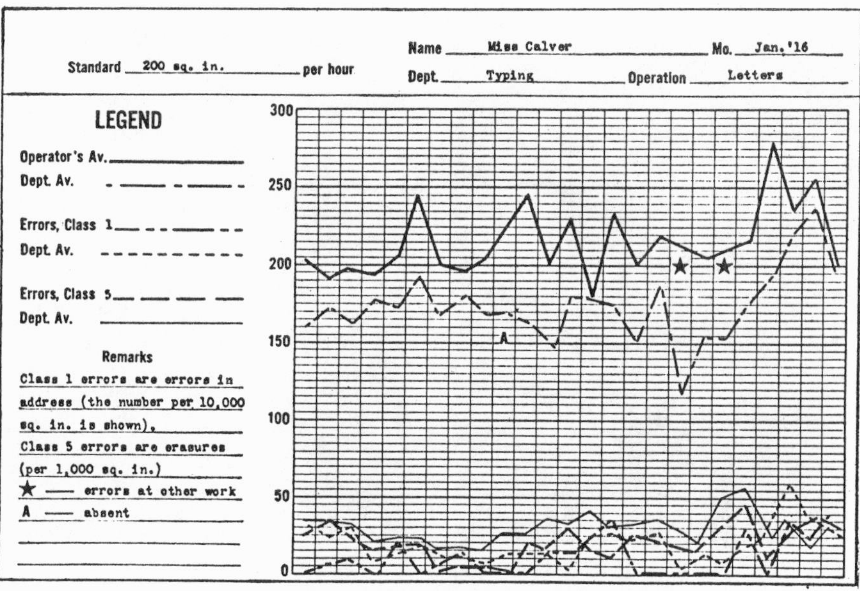

-AND AFTER FOUR MONTHS' TRAINING

As an incentive to the girls to do good work, the management promises to give them cards like this if they wish to leave the company, in place of a letter of recommendation. This card illustrates again (see page 462) the fact that errors do not increase proportionally with increased speed

made preparations to establish a bonus system. We did not undertake to do this, however, until all external hindrances had been removed and each operator studied and her faults corrected as far as possible. Sound management does not set a merely theoretical standard, such as could be attained by none but the most experienced operators. Once a standard rate has been set it should not be changed unless the methods are also changed. It was therefore important to exercise great care in setting a standard which, while difficult to attain, should not be impossible. Had we taken the observations in the beginning and set a standard then it would have been fair neither to the worker nor the company.

What we did, therefore, was to take a large number of tests on a standard piece of copy. These tests were taken at all hours of the day, and a number of tests taken on different days for each girl. Several weeks were required for completing these studies. We then made studies of each individual motion – (1) inserting the paper in the machine; (2) reading and copying address; (3) reading and typewriting copy; (4) taking the paper out of the machine, – and so on.

Next, we took many tests on miscellaneous copy, and the results were averaged with the first tests. Finally, half-hourly tests were taken during the whole day on a number of the operators.

All of the operations which were repeated, such as getting paper, inserting it in the machine, taking it out of the machine, and so on, were taken from the lowest figures in the time studies. We reasoned that all could be taught to do these operations in the most efficient

THE RIGHT POSITION - - AND THE WRONG

A typist's position at her machine, Mr. Leffingwell's experience shows, has a great deal to do with whether or not she feels tired at the end of the day

The photograph at the left shows the position which causes least fatigue according to Mr. Leffingwell's experience. The one at the right is a common posture, and will quickly tire a girl

manner. The operation of typewriting copy was averaged, after eliminating the records of those who were hopelessly slow. On the other hand, the highest averages were not taken here as a standard, but lumped with the others. We found that 250 square inches per hour was a theoretical possibility with the operators then working. A deduction of 20 per cent was made for unavoidable delays, and a standard of 200 square inches per hour set.

It is one thing to set the standard and quite another thing to get it done, not once, but steadily every day.

Most of the typists were beginners, though some had several years' experience. The wages ranged from $7 to $15 per week. We fixed a standard wage of $9.50 for convenience in figuring the bonus. This standard did not change the regular wages of the operators in any way. If, however, a girl reached the standard of 200 square inches per hour for the length of time she was working upon a standardized operation, she got a bonus of 10 cents per hour. If she worked the entire week of 47½ hours at standard speed, this amounted to $4.75. She got this bonus, whether her salary was $7 or $15.

The bonus was paid on a sliding scale, as follows:

Sq. in. per hr.	Bonus per hr.	Sq. in. per hr.	Bonus per hr.
136	$0.0020	170	$0.0280
138	.0028	172	.0300
140	.0040	174	.0320
142	.0056	176	.0340
144	.0068	178	.0360
146	.0088	180	.0400
148	.0104	182	.0440
150	.0120	184	.0480
152	.0132	186	.0520
154	.0148	188	.0560
156	.0160	190	.0600
158	.0176	192	.0640
160	.0200	194	.0680
162	.0208	196	.0720
164	.0224	198	.0760
166	.0240	200	.1000
168	.0260	220	.1400
		240	.1800

It was understood that no operator would lose her position because she was unable to reach the standard. The only penalty would be no bonus money in the pay envelope.

HOW THE OPERATORS WERE TRAINED TO REACH THE STANDARD OUTPUT

At first, none of the girls believed it was possible to attain the standard. As the average number of square inches per hour when the records were first kept was eighty, and this had gradually climbed up to one hundred and twenty-seven, it is not surprising that they thought the standard too high.

For several weeks no one earned any bonus, though considerable effort was put forth.

Then we made rest and fatigue studies. One of the best and most faithful workers was selected for these studies. Records were taken by half-hour periods. The operator was first kept at work at a high speed during the entire day. At another time she was given five minutes rest every hour, and every other hour a rest of ten minutes. The results of these studies proved conclusively that four hours is too long a period to expect a typist to remain at the machine and do rapid and good work.

Recess periods were therefore established as follows: one ten-minute recess in the morning at 10:30 and another in the afternoon at 3:30. During these recess periods the windows were thrown open and all employees encouraged to go outside and play. Later on, employees were allowed five minutes before recess and five minutes after recess, both in the morning and afternoon, this time to be taken at their own convenience. Thus employees now have forty minutes of rest a day in a working day of eight and one-half hours. That this pays the company is evident from the charts accompanying this article.

However, although the bonus plan had been in operation for several weeks, and although the output had increased considerably, no one succeeded in reaching the standard. The girls all insisted that the standard was too high.

At about this time one of the girls who had been below the average in speed was offered a prize of one dollar for the first hour she reached the standard. The very next day she came down to work determined to win that dollar. After several hours spent in the attempt, she won the prize. That broke the ice. It *was* possible, after all. The same prize was offered to all the girls in the department and thereafter, day after day, one after another won it until finally reaching the standard became a habit.

It is a prevalent idea that one can not work rapidly and accurately. The reverse is proved by all of our experience. In order to do rapid work, one must do careful and accurate work. It is a fact that almost amounts to a law. From the beginning, our employees were penalized heavily for errors. The chart on page 462 shows how the errors went down as the product increased. In typewriting, as in many other lines of work, it has been proved that in order to do rapid work one must concentrate. And this in itself decreases the chance of error.

The very first attempt at increased speed, indeed, usually means an increase in errors, simply because the operator is straining herself to make a record. She is just a little bit doubtful as to whether or not she can attain the standard. But as she gains confidence, the errors gradually diminish until finally she has a much lower record of errors at the high speed than she had at the low speed. This statement is made only after carefully tabulating and charting thousands of observations.

SOME POINTS TO REMEMBER IN AIMING AT INCREASED OUTPUT

In this connection, it is perhaps well to emphasize the importance of confidence. It is important at all times that the worker be encouraged and coached, just exactly as an athlete is. An employee must never be scolded for not reaching the standard, nor accused of "stalling." Once let her get the idea that she is being driven, and the chance for really effective work is destroyed. Almost always, I have found, more can be done by coaxing than by driving.

A word might also be said about office discipline. We have but little use for that word now. Another word – cooperation – has more effect with us. Each worker is permitted to choose her own code of ethics. The result of not attending to business – gossiping, "stalling," being tardy, absent, or doing any or all of the hundred and one other little things that often lower output in offices – is simply less bonus. That is punishment enough. Employees in our office are constantly seeking work – not an opportunity to get out of it. During the recess their natural desire to talk, laugh and play is satisfied – the rest of the time work is the order of the day.

By these methods the effectiveness of the entire typist department has been brought up from an average of 80 square inches per hour to nearly 200 square inches; and on several occasions the output has run over that figure. The average of some of the girls for an entire week has exceeded 230 square inches. One operator has reached an average of 278 square inches for one day.

I have confined my remarks to the typing of letters. But we handle several different kinds of work. The standard for typewriting envelopes from hand written copy is two hundred per hour. The standard for typewriting envelopes from typewritten copy is two hundred and forty per hour. The same bonus rate and standard wage applies on all standardized operations in the department.

A careful daily record is kept of the work of each employee, showing the amount done, the number of errors, attendance, tardiness, and so on. This information is daily charted upon a card by months, as shown in the illustrations on pages 464 and 465, and becomes a graphic record of the employee's work during the entire period of her employment.

Recently the management has announced to the employees that if at any time they find it to their advantage to leave the employ of the company, they will be given a copy of their graph cards for use in securing another position. It can readily be seen what valuable recommendations some of the cards will be. Even more interesting, perhaps, is the confidence thus shown by the company in its ability to hold its employees.

In next month's issue of SYSTEM, I shall continue this story of the reorganization of our office and show how we applied the principles of the Taylor system of scientific management to our office work.

WHAT "SCIENTIFIC MANAGEMENT" DID FOR MY OFFICE

William H. Leffingwell

THIRD IN A SERIES DETAILING THE SAVINGS SECURED BY REORGANIZING AN OFFICE

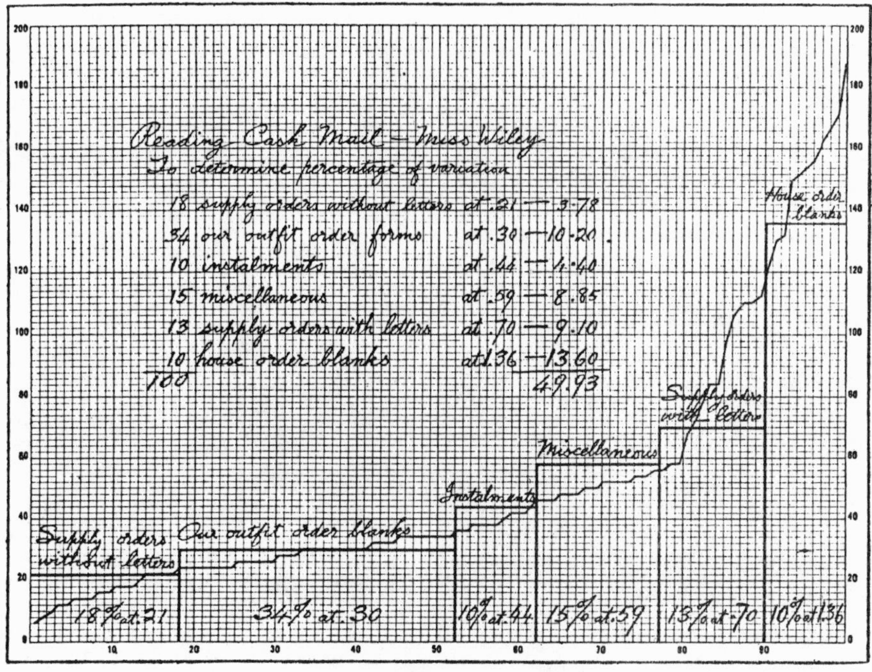

CHARTING A TIME STUDY

In the office as well as in the factory, Mr. Leffingwell points out in this article, stop watch studies may be advantageously used to determine the standard time a given task should take. Above is shown the graphic record of one such study. The reverse of this sheet, giving complete details, is illustrated on page 619

WHAT "SCIENTIFIC MANAGEMENT" DID FOR MY OFFICE

BY WM. H. LEFFINGWELL *Illustrated with* PHOTOGRAPHS *and* FORMS

HOW we applied the Taylor system of scientific management to our office work will probably be interesting to others who have come in contact with the ordinary conditions under which office work is performed. Ours is an instalment business and most of our sales are made through following up by mail the inquiries we receive in reply to our advertisements. The office operations are quite similar to those carried on in other offices. For instance, when the advertising and the follow-up result in sales, we have to ship the goods, and at the same time record the transactions so as to collect our money as the instalments come due.

There are five monthly instalments. When everything goes according to schedule, we have to handle each customer's account from seven to ten times, every handling involving from five to ten clerical operations. Thus, before we have finished with a customer we have performed anywhere from thirty-five to one hundred clerical operations. If the customer fails to pay on the scheduled time, there are still more operations. It is true that some of these operations require only a small amount of time, but they are operations nevertheless, and must be performed.

As an illustration, I shall take the simple case of receiving a letter from a prospect who answered one of our advertisements. These operations are necessary:

1. Open mail;
2. Read;
3. Type record of inquiry;
4. Type form letter of reply;
5. Fold circulars;
6. Fold letter;
7. Enclose letter and circular in envelope;
8. Stamp and mail.

If he does not respond with an order within a reasonable length of time, the last five of the above operations must be repeated on a follow-up. In some cases we send a third and a fourth follow-up, on which, of course, the same operations have to be repeated.

Now, suppose the prospect does respond with an order. The following operations have to be performed:

1. Open mail;
2. Verify cash, if any;
3. Stamp letter with date of arrival;
4. Register the order;
5. Credit the source of inquiry for our advertising records;
6. Interpret the order;
7. Decide how to ship it;
8. Make an invoice;
9. Make a shipping record;
10. Address a label;
11. Acknowledge the order with a form letter;
12. Enclose acknowledgment letter and invoice;
13. Stamp and mail letter;
14. Make a record on our card ledger of the account.

The work of gathering, packing and shipping the goods is not included in the office work and so need not be classified.

DISTRIBUTING DEPARTMENT MAIL

Here is a convenient rack specially designed so the girl can speedily distribute mail for the various departments. There is a separate folder on the rack for each department

If the customer pays each instalment as it becomes due, it is necessary on five different occasions to perform the following operations:

1. Open letter containing the remittance;
2. Verify cash;
3. Find his account;
4. Credit it.

If he fails to pay promptly, it is necessary to perform a set of four other operations, as follows:

1. Find his account;
2. Address and type a form letter dun;
3. Enclose it in envelope;
4. Stamp and mail.

In some cases, several letters have to be sent to collect just one remittance, so this last set of operations may be repeated several times.

This brief explanation of our problem does not cover

all the ramifications of the work by any means; but it is sufficient to suggest the problems we had to consider. Probably corresponding conditions would be found in other offices through similar analyses.

Certain of the operations mentioned naturally fall into departments. For example, all mail has to be opened, no matter what its destination, and all letters may be made from one department. Typewriting is the same, whether it is typing form letters or addressing envelopes, or answering correspondence. So we established a separate typists' department.

THIS CABINET SAVES REACHING

Special equipment to fit the work helped increase the output of Mr. Leffingwell's typists. Here, for example, is a cabinet to hold invoice forms, which saves unnecessary reaching and leaves the desk free for the orders that are being copied

The first step in the work was to standardize. The incoming mail, we found, was of six classes:

1. Executive office mail;
2. Inquiries from prospective customers;
3. Letters containing money and orders and general correspondence;
4. C. O. D. remittances from express companies and the post office;
5. Post card notices from express companies;
6. Newspapers and magazines containing proofs of the insertion of our advertisements.

It was a simple matter to distinguish these letters before they were opened, and we found it saved time to do so. Letters in the first class were easily detected by the corner card, or quite often they were addressed to some member of the firm or an executive. These were separated at once and sent to the executive offices, mostly unopened.

Letters in the second class bore our advertising "key" on the envelope. These letters seldom contained more than the coupon from the paper. The letters in the third class proved our real problem, for these letters contained money, orders and correspondence that needed immediate attention. They were usually in our return envelopes and could easily be picked out. Letters in the fourth, fifth and sixth classes did not require immediate attention, and they were set aside until all other letters had received attention.

This sorting of the mail was a helpful preliminary step towards standardizing, for it enabled all departments to start work on the day's mail without delay. To get a further start, we had the employees of the mail opening department come to work a half hour earlier than the rest of the office, so that by the time the clerks arrived a part of the mail was opened and ready for work to begin.

After the cash was taken out of the letters and properly recorded, study showed us that the letters flowed in three streams. The first stream was composed of orders, the second of payments on account and the third was correspondence of various sorts.

If there had never been cross-currents in these three streams, our problem would have been simple. But it is impossible to control the actions of customers. They often mixed the streams up considerably. Some letters would contain perhaps a complaint, a remittance on account and an order, all scrawled in pencil, in scarcely legible handwriting, and covering five or six pages.

This made it necessary to subdivide the mail into two streams: (1) "cash," and (2) "no money enclosed." This latter stream was again divided into "orders" and "correspondence." It can be seen that both the "cash" and "no money enclosed" mail required careful reading by some one thoroughly acquainted with the business. The training of the clerks in this department has been described in the article which appeared in the October issue of SYSTEM.

It was clear to us that if suitable records were to be had of orders it would be necessary to keep them in various ways: (1) by shipping date, (2) numerically, and (3) alphabetically by states. It was also necessary for these records to be accurate, a condition which required careful inspection before shipments were allowed to leave the house.

The ordinary way of keeping these records, including making out the invoices and the labels, would have meant that each name would have to be written at least five times. That would give us five chances to make errors. This difficulty we obviated by making the original invoice on the typewriter with a duplicating ribbon, and duplicating it upon all five records with mechanical duplicators.

It would be impossible in the space of an article to describe all the details of how we standardized our methods. What we did was carefully to list all of the necessary steps, and then study them with a view to finding the one best method of accomplishing our purpose, using mechanical means wherever possible. When this one best method was found, it was standardized, written out and taught to our employees.

We next proceeded to standardize the equipment. By this I do not mean that we got the same kind of desks for everyone. On the contrary, we studied the requirements of each class of work and got special equipment for each class.

SHEET NO. **DAILY CASH RECEIPTS** DATE ________

NUMBER	STAMPS	CASH	AUDIT CHECK	NAME	ADDRESS	STATE	INSTALMENT C. O. D.	INSTALMENT	SPECIAL C. O. D.	SUPPLY	PROFESSIONAL	UNAPPLIED	SPECIAL	ACCOUNT	AUDIT CHECK
50		5 00		A. F. Leach	Washington, R. F. D. 3	S. D.		5.00							
51		1 00		S. E. Deane	Beryl Hills	Wyo.		1.00							
52		4 00		F. J. Deming	N. Y. City	N. Y.				4.00					
53		5 50	✓	C. E. Moore	Columbus, 1718 Broad St.	O.	5.50								
54	1.00			Chas. Miller	Chicago, 1720 Barker Ave.	Ill.			1.00						
55		4 00	✓	F. B. Caswell	Jefferson City	Mich.			4.00						
56		2 00	✓	C. B. Case	Windy City, R. F. D. 1	Ill.		2.00							
97															
98															
99															
TOTAL STAMPS GRAND TOTAL															

BALANCED BY | LISTED BY | MAIL READER | CHECKED BY

TOTAL CHECKS ________
" CURRENCY ________
" CASH ________
" STAMPS ________
GRAND TOTAL ________

NO. INSTALMENT ITEMS ________
" SPECIAL C. O. D. ________
TOTAL ________

NO. PROFESSIONAL ITEMS ________
" UNAPPLIED ________
" SPECIAL ________

SHEET NO. ________
DATE ________

KEEPING TRACK OF INCOMING CASH

On sheets like this the cashier notes the sums received in the mail, in the columns at the left. Later a typist fills in the names and addresses and credits the proper accounts. The sheet number and the position which any order takes on the sheet, combined, give that order its permanent number

For the most part these were simple additions to tables and drawers such as a carpenter or "handy man" could install for us.

For example, the mail readers had to divide the mail into several different classes. We made a simple rack with partitions, so that the work could be easily and quickly sorted. For the invoice typists we had a simple cabinet built over their typewriters so that the invoice blanks could be reached with a minimum of effort and the desk space left free to hold the orders they were copying. The mail opening department, again, had special pigeon holes for distributing the envelopes.

Originally, there were several kinds of typewriter desks in use with us. All of these except one kind were abandoned. There were half a dozen kinds and sizes of other desks and tables. These we junked and substituted plain, simple tables that served the purpose much better when they had the added specially-built equipment we felt we needed put on them.

The office itself we laid out on a plan which enabled the work to proceed from one end to the other in a continuous line.

Once we discovered the best method of doing an operation, we taught this method to all who were doing that particular work. Then we recorded the method on sheets, so that this standard way could be perpetuated, no matter how often the clerks changed. We had, in addition to the "policy book" that was described in a previous article,* a book of general office instructions and special instructions for each class of work. As far as possible, every step was put in writing.

At the same time that we were carrying on this standardization work, we were also taking time and motion studies in order to find the best methods. The exact method of making an office time study may be interesting and I shall describe a typical case, which happens to consist of finding the best way to "read

THE PLANNING BOARD

Pins of various colors are placed opposite employees' names on this board to show how much work they have on their desks. The planning clerk divides the incoming work among the various employees accordingly

cash mail," and arriving at a standard task. I am not describing our method of handling the cash as in any way novel or unusual, but merely take it to show the way the time study was handled and what is necessary in order to set a standard.

In the mail opening department, then, the money is separated from the letters, the envelope is opened on three sides and is attached to the letter. The envelope is

*In the October issue of SYSTEM, page 373.

then stamped with a rubber stamp. At the proper place in the record the cashier marks in blue pencil the amount of money received.

The cashier makes no effort to find out what the money is for—this would delay the work too long. So she uses a special "daily cash receipts" sheet (see page 616). This sheet bears a folio number.

HOW THE ORDERS ARE PUT ON THE RECORDS

Now, each piece of mail is stamped with the money stamp, and a number. The first three figures of the number correspond with the folio number on the "daily cash receipts" sheet. The last two are the individual number for that particular receipt.

Thus, 13698 would mean that the item was number 98 on folio number 136. This identifies the remittance for all future references. The sheets are in pairs and are numbered from 00 to 49 and from 50 to 99. After the cashier has marked in blue pencil, in the proper space on the envelope, the amount of the remittance, she writes in the amount of each remittance on the correct line on the numbered cash sheet.

Each sheet then contains the figures representing the amounts of the remittances only, opposite the respective numbers. There are just fifty items to a sheet. After the cashier has balanced the cash with this cash sheet, the sheet is sent first to a cash mail reader, who reads the letters and decides what the money is for; then it goes to a typist, who lists the names and addresses and inserts the amount of the remittance in the proper column or columns.

It will be readily understood that there are many variations in the work of the cash mail reader. For example, if a letter contains a complaint, an order for supplies and a payment on account, it is necessary to send some of this information to the ledger department to have the customer credited with the payment; some more of it to the correspondence department to have his complaint answered and the rest of it to the order department to have the order filled.

To send the original letter to each of these three departments in succession would cause too much delay. So the order is copied off on a "house order blank," and the customer's name and address and the amount of money paid on account shown on the envelope. The letter is marked "order detached and sent to the correspondence department." Thus, each department gets busy at about the same time.

We have discovered that there are many little distinctive phrases, such as the readers' instructions, interpretations, suggestions, and the like, which are written many times during the day. These we have classified and put on rubber stamps, which save a lot of writing.

In spite of all this standardization, however, we found there was still a great deal of variation in the work. Some items would require from one to two minutes to handle, others not more than .15 of a minute.

DECIDING HOW LONG IT SHOULD TAKE TO ANSWER A LETTER

So we timed these variations carefully with a decimal time study stop watch. Finally it was possible for us to classify six different kinds of letters that required different times for handling. The average time for each kind of letter we obtained by taking several hundred studies until we could almost predict with certainty the amount of time necessary. Each girl was then given a score card and for several days kept a careful record of the number of letters she received under each of these six classifications. This gave us roughly the percentage of each class of letter, and from then on it was a simple matter of arithmetic to set the correct standards.

The nature of the work, being so varied, did not make for great speed, and it was a

TIME STUDY

Date 5/15/16

Name of Operator Miss Wiley
Study Taken by N. R. Engel
Time of Day Taken 2:35 p.m.
Purpose of Study To determine % of variation

Name of Operation Reading Cash Mail
Tools Used Blue Pencil — Rubber Stamps
Machine Used
Read and Approved by Leffingwell

NO.	Motion or Operation	Continuous Time	Individual Time	Continuous Time	Individual Time	Continuous Time	Individual Time	Continuous Time	Individual Time
1	Take up	.20	✓ .20	* 12.36	✓ .12	.17	✓ .17	C 1309	.33
2	Read	C 75	✓ .55	* 12.62	✓ .26	I .70	✓ .53	* 1322	.13
3		C .96	✓ .21	C 12.95	✓ .33	S2/2.41	✓ 1.71	COD 1360	.38
4		C 1.26	✓ .30	C 13.43	✓ .48	S 2.71	✓ .30	* 13.70	.10
5		S 1.89	✓ .63	C 13.80	✓ .37	C 2.93	✓ 22	C 14.00	.30
6		S 2.46	✓ .57	S2/14.91	✓ 1.11	P2/4.45	✓ 1.52	C 14.26	.26
7		I2/3.44	✓ .98	C 15.43	✓ .52	C 4.76	✓ .31	I 15.36	1.10
8		C2/3.86	✓ .42	COD 15.66	✓ .23	C 5.03	✓ .27	S 15.85	.49
9		C2/4.16	✓ .30	IC 16.49	✓ .83	* 5.27	✓ .24	C 16.17	.32
10		C 4.62	✓ .46	S 16.77	✓ .28	P 5.60	✓ .33	S2/17.27	1.10
11		C 4.81	✓ .19	S2/18.44	✓ 1.67	* 5.93	✓ .33	* 17.46	.19
12		S 5.12	✓ .31	C 18.69	✓ .25	* 6.31	✓ .38	S 19.03	1.67
13		C 5.48	✓ .36	I 18.76	✓ .07	P2/7.60	✓ 1.29	* 19.12	.09
14		C 5 70	✓ .22	I 19.26	✓ .50	C 7.90	✓ .30	S 20.19	1.07
15		* 5.88	✓ .18	C 19.79	✓ .53	I 8.10	✓ .20	C 20.65	.46
16		* 6.05	✓ .17	C2/21.11	✓ 1.32	COD 8.65	✓ 55	C 20.87	.22
17		* 6.13	✓ .08	C 21.35	✓ .24	C 8.86	✓ 21	C 21.08	.21
18		S 6.84	✓ .71	* 21.69	✓ 34	C 9.11	✓ 25	* 21.25	.17
19		S2/8.38	✓ 1.54	C 21.97	✓ .28	I 9.54	✓ .43	COD 21.55	.30
20		S 8.84	✓ .46	* 22.34	✓ .37	C 10.07	✓ .53	C 22.05	.50
21		I 9.20	✓ .36	I 22.92	✓ .58	C 10.32	✓ .25	I 22.27	.22
22		C 9.53	✓ .33	S2/23.71	✓ 79	S 10.62	✓ 30	C2/23.11	84
23		C 9.86	✓ .33	* 24.11	✓ .40	C 10.85	✓ 23	C2/24.99	1.88
24		* 9.97	✓ .11	C 24.70	✓ .59	C 11.08	✓ 23	COD 25.20	.21
25		✓ 11.58	✓ 1.61	I 25.12	✓ 42	✓ 11.56	.48	* 25 31	.11
	Finish	S 12.24	Finish .66	25.60	.48	S 12.76	1.20	25.72	.41

Remarks: C — Our outfit order blanks. S — Supply order with letter. * — Supply order without letter. Z — House order blank. I — Instalment

HOW THE TIME STUDIES ARE RECORDED

On a sheet like this the time study man records the name of the operation and the exact time of performing it. Usually 50 or more studies are made before deciding on the standard time. The reverse of this sheet is illustrated on page 613

simple matter for a clerk to show all appearances of being diligently performing her work, when as a matter of fact she was not accomplishing half the work she should. No amount of watching would have discovered this. As a matter of fact, with two girls who were working side by side, we found that one did fifty per cent more than the other. The slow one said: "I have all of the 'stickers.'" Before we set standards, we had no means of disproving her statement. When the standards were finally set, it was just double the average performance. Then we began the training necessary to get the task set accomplished.

Decision is the most important factor in this work, so we told the girls to practice making quick decisions. After several weeks of training the standard was reached, and on some occasions passed. Previously it took just as long to do this work on the slack days as it did on the busy ones.

The accompanying time study sheet (pages 613 and 619) shows both the method of actually taking the study and the graphic method of interpreting it. It happens to be one of the later studies made on the operation just described. We have continued practically the same method of taking time studies throughout the work, and newer and better methods are constantly being found.

In classifying and arriving at percentages of variables, the employees themselves always take the score. Their record is compared with the score taken by the time study man. By this method, the percentages can be arrived at for a comparatively low cost and are quite accurate, since the employees do not know to what use their scores are put. We carefully preserve and classify our time study sheets.

GETTING THE GIRLS TO PERFORM THE STANDARD TASKS

I have found it usually desirable to take from fifty to one hundred studies in order to arrive at a definite standard. In taking these studies, the time study man watches closely for variations in the methods used, and very often discovers the reason why it takes one operator longer than another. This leads to rapid improvements.

After the standard has once been set, and the time required for each motion is known, the time study man assists the employee in reaching the standard by pointing out just where she is slow, and showing her how she can improve her work. It has been my experience that most employees really want to reach the standard and are anxious to have whatever assistance they can get to enable them to do so.

Corresponding with the "functional foremen" in factories, we have in our office the following employees:

Time study men, who also act as teachers on some mechanical operations;

Teachers for all operations requiring decision. These teachers are usually the best workers in the department on the particular operation involved. They know the work thoroughly. Except with new employees, it is not necessary that this instruction be carried on all the time, so it costs but little;

Order of work clerks: It is the duty of certain clerks in the various departments, and of one clerk in the planning department, to see that the work is kept moving and does not become congested at any one place. If an employee falls behind for any reason, the work is not permitted to be left undone, but some other employee is shifted over to assist at that particular point;

A time clerk, who computes the bonuses.

These "functional foremen" relieve the department managers of a great deal of work which they are usually compelled to do. Besides, that work is handled much better, since it is done for the benefit of the whole establishment and not for the special benefit of a particular department.

The planning department has already been mentioned. It has many duties of a staff or advisory nature, but its chief function is to see that work is done carefully in the order planned, and that employees are performing their prescribed tasks not only from day to day, but every hour.

This department schedules the regular work of all departments, and special jobs of every kind. It is thoroughly understood that the planning department has no authority to interfere with the management of any department. It can only suggest or advise that work be done in a certain manner or by a certain clerk. So successful, in fact, has it been in our plant that all department managers lean heavily upon the planning department and find that it makes their work of supervision much easier.

HOW THE PLANNING DEPARTMENT DIRECTS THE WORK

Its functions may be briefly described as twofold, as follows:

(1) Research work, such as discovering the one best method, improving equipment, improving conditions of working, recording and classifying best methods, best equipment, and so on;

(2) Detail work: getting the regular and special details accomplished in the best and quickest manner.

This department also keeps records of accomplishment and makes charts for each employee, similar to the one described in the article which appeared in the November issue of SYSTEM. Charts are also made for the bulletin board, showing graphically the best accomplishments.

The idea here, of course, is to excite the emulation of others.

The planning department also keeps on file catalogs of all office equipment and labor-saving devices, and has a card index, thoroughly cross indexed. Special articles in magazines, periodicals or books bearing upon our problems, and which we might have occasion to use at some future time, are carefully indexed by volumes and pages.

HOW THE "AUTOMATIC MEMORY" OF THE OFFICE OPERATES

In this department we have also our "memory clerk"—an employee who, with about half an hour's work a day, keeps a much more effective tickler system for the entire office than is sometimes found in offices where every executive keeps his own tickler. The method is simple. Any one who wishes to use the tickler system makes some such rough memorandum as "Remind me on June 14, at 9:00 o'clock, to . . . ." He then signs his name.

This memorandum is sent to the "memory clerk." She files it away to reappear on June 14. If it is of a confidential nature, the owner encloses it in an envelope. The first duty of the "memory clerk" each morning is to tear off the date on the office calendar. At that time she consults the tickler for tickler notes which have been placed in the files to come up on that date.

The system is extensively used by all departments for follow-ups of all sorts. For example, if a department manager gives certain instructions to his employees one day, and wishes to look into the question again in a few days or a week to see if the orders are being followed, he merely sends a note to the "memory clerk," and in the due course of time is reminded to check up.

This file is also used for planning the work ahead when sending out follow-up letters. For example, if we receive five thousand inquiries today, an unusually large number, we must follow them up again in ten days. The number of inquiries received is placed ahead eight days, or if the number received is exceptionally large, six days. Then, six days later, let us say, we are reminded that we have an exceptional number of follow-up letters to get out, and we can prepare for them. Thus the follow-up is never delayed for so trivial a reason as the fact that we did not know there would be so many letters to handle.

The use of this tickler system, in fact, is very general and serves a large number of purposes. During six months' operation, the "memory clerk" has not failed once. The work has become practically automatic.

Routing the work through the office is also one of the duties of the planning department. Our planning board is a simple affair, which we have ruled with vertical lines to indicate the hours of the day, and with horizontal lines for the names of employees. We use pins of various colors which enable the department to keep track of the work of all employees.

First of all, the work is divided into units. The amount of time each clerk or typist should take to perform a certain unit of work is known in advance; and, as the work is given out to the various employees, pins are placed ahead on the planning board accordingly.

This enables us to not only plan the work at once for the first operation, but also for the very last one. The board shows at all times not only how much work a clerk has on his or her desk, but as well how much is in the house and due to come to the desk later on. Thus, possible congestion is foreseen, and usually can be avoided. A photograph of the board is shown on page 617.

Other details connected with our installation of the methods characteristic of "scientific management" in our office will have to go over until the next article, which will appear in the January issue of SYSTEM.

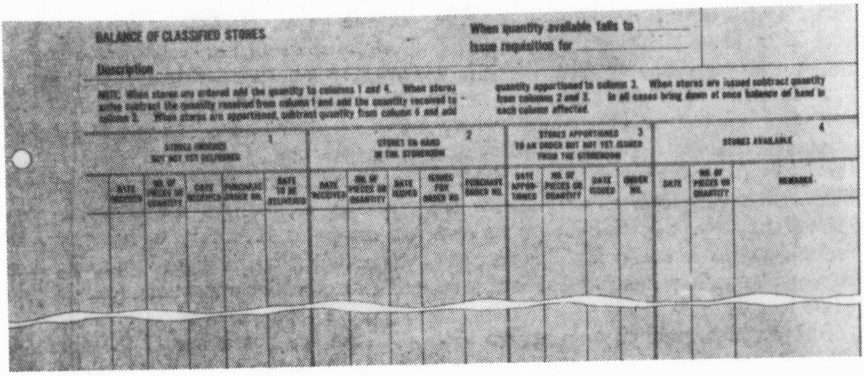

FOURTH IN A SERIES DESCRIBING THE SAVINGS SECURED BY REORGANIZING AN OFFICE

MAKING RE-ORDERS AUTOMATIC

A perpetual inventory of each kind of stationery used in the office is kept on a record like this. The record does away with such difficulties as rush orders, oversupplies, or exhaustion of the supply at a critical moment and makes the job of re-ordering simple

WHAT "SCIENTIFIC MANAGEMENT" DID FOR MY OFFICE

By WM. H. LEFFINGWELL — *Illustrated with* PHOTOGRAPHS

LAST month I described some of the steps we took to apply the principles of the Taylor system of scientific management to office work, and mentioned a few of the results we secured. The space available ran out before I finished my description of these methods. So in this article I shall complete the story of our work and its results.

One of the prominent features of the Taylor system is the setting of tasks. This we have found perhaps the most valuable feature in our work. Mr. Taylor mentions four fundamental rules for efficient work, as follows:

First, a large daily task
Second, standard conditions
Third, high pay for success
Fourth, loss in case of failure

It may perhaps be argued that there is nothing new in the task idea. As a matter of fact, there is nothing new in the idea itself; but when it comes to the question of application, probably there are few offices that have actually put it in operation. In some places, indeed, records are kept of the amount of work done; but no task is set, ordinarily, and the "good" employees are those who do the most work. In my experience, however, I have found it true that the "best" girl in an office may be doing only half of what she is capable of doing under proper guidance. So the problem is plainly worth study.

The work of setting tasks must be done scientifically. First, know the task is possible of accomplishment; second, know it is a good day's work. To set a task scientifically, therefore, requires patient observation and investigation.

Nothing is so detrimental to real effectiveness, I have found, as setting a task either too high or too low. If it is too high, the employees will do very little more than they have been accustomed to accomplishing previously, simply in order to show the management how impossible of achievement the expected task is. If it is too low, on the other hand, they may fear to do as much as they are really capable of doing. However, a standard may be much higher than current output and still not be too high, provided it has been carefully set and the employees are patiently and thoroughly taught to perform the work at the high standard.

It requires considerable diplomacy to get a worker to perform a task which is very much higher than he has been accustomed to doing. First of all, it must be explained to him that the secret does not lie so much in working rapidly, as in making every motion count and working all the time. It is usually a blow to the pride of any worker if you tell him that he is doing only half as much as he should.

It is also ridiculous to set tasks and expect them to be performed if other factors outside of the control of the individual worker interfere with effective work. For example, it is folly to expect maximum output if the worker is kept waiting for work.

WHAT IS THE BEST WAY TO GET THE STANDARD TASK PERFORMED?

After the task has been set, I have found it important to let employees know you are interested in their efforts to accomplish it. They must know daily, sometimes hourly, just how much they are doing. Constant attention and assistance is necessary in some instances for weeks and, occasionally, months. I never discharge an employee simply for failing to accomplish the task. Such an event would cause demoralization at once and create in the minds of the rest of the employees a suspicion that the company was "working them to death." I always assume that an employee is doing his best. If it becomes apparent that he is not making an effort, or can not reach the standard, I transfer him to some other work for which he may be better fitted.

The best way to get a task done, I am convinced, is to work patiently with one employee until he has attained the mark set. This then shows the others that the task is possible, and one by one the majority will reach the standard. Those who do not are either incapable or indifferent. If the latter, much can usually be done by tactfully assuming that there must be some reason – not the fault of the employee – why he is not doing so well as the others. No one likes to feel that he is incompetent. If there are any grievances or genuine drawbacks they are likely to be advanced at once.

I have used many ways of getting a task done. In one case I purposely chose the employee with the lowest record, and coached her with all the care and enthusiasm of an athletic trainer. I backed her to win "over the whole bunch." Naturally, this aroused her latent pride.

At first the others looked on with considerable amusement. Some of the better girls seemed to think it was like trying to make a racer out of a dray horse. But when the slow one began to improve, I had her daily record posted. The others worked harder than usual, so as not to give her all the glory. It became a contest and in a very short time the slow girl was in the lead with the others making desperate efforts to follow. Finally, when she had reached the standard set – which, by the way, was three and one third times as much as she did at first – all coaching on her was discontinued and it took only a short time to bring the whole department up to the standard. The slow girl did not lose her speed, and she has jealously guarded her new record.

On another occasion, after several days of patient teaching, a young man persisted in making a large number of useless motions. I walked up to him unexpectedly, grasped his hand and held it for the time usually occupied by his useless motions. Then I pointed out the result. I had not interfered with his work.

THE WRONG WAY

One of the methods of "scientific management" is to provide equipment that will enable the worker to perform operations with the fewest motions. The distribution file pictured above is poorly planned. The clerk has to walk from end to end of the files, and reach far above her head to some of the bins

He grasped the point and one or two days thereafter reached the standard. So well had he learned that the best work is accomplished by a minimum of motions that he studied his job intently and soon with very little effort earned the maximum bonus given for 120 per cent effectiveness. Formerly he had become tired out trying to perform 50 per cent of the task set.

In other cases, where it was apparent that the task could be attained if the desire to reach it was strong enough, I have offered a prize of one dollar to the first clerk who reaches the standard for one hour. To get a dollar for one hour's work is sufficient inducement to arouse the energy of almost any clerk. In such cases it rarely happens that the prize is not won within a few days. Once some one has reached the standard the ice is broken. It is no longer a question of whether or not it can be done.

Another point which we have adopted from "scientific management" is the use of mnemonic, or easily remembered symbols, for departments, forms and jobs. The method has proved much more satisfactory than the usual method of using numbers or letters in a more or less haphazard way. I will explain briefly how we have used the mnemonic method.

In planning our system we first put down all the letters in the alphabet and then filled in opposite each the name of that department the initial letter of the name of which was best represented by that letter in the alphabet. This necessitated re-naming some departments in order not to have certain letters repeated. Our classification is as follows:

A Auditing department
B Bookkeeping department
C Correspondence department
D Duplicator department
E Employment department
F Factory
G General manager
I Inspection department
L Ledger department (customer's card)
M Mail opening department
O Order department
P Purchasing department
R Returned goods and receiving department
S Sales department (advertising)
T Typewriting department

We still had the following departments left over, unnamed:

Collection
Planning
Shipping
Mailing

We compromised by spelling collection with a k – kollection. We took the last letter of plan – n. As most of our shipping was done by express (xpress) we called the shipping department "X." The mailing department was called "U" after Uncle Sam. It is customary in similar instances to use a distinctive second letter. Thus we might have let "PU" mean purchasing department and "PL" mean planning department. Our reason for not doing so was that we wished to have the first capital letter in a symbol indicate a department, and the second capital letter a subdivision of that department, or one of its special functions. Thus, "CC" means the claim division of the correspondence department.

We also established a rule that the small letters would represent forms. Small letters were never used alone, but always following a department symbol. If it happens that a number of different forms would logically all bear the same symbol (it rarely happens that there are more than a few of a kind), we use numbers after the symbols. Thus, Ob-1 and Ob-2 indicate the bills or invoices, numbered 1 and 2, used in the order department.

There is no difficulty in remembering a symbol of this sort and it leads to classifications of a common sense sort.

One interesting by-product of preparing for the installation of the mnemonic system was our discovery of many forms and pieces of stationery that had been discontinued and forgotten. They were entirely useless. These we had carried in our storage bins, in some cases for years, taking up valuable space that was badly needed. Had we not made an attempt to classify the stationery according to departments and uses, these now discarded forms might be there still.

The stores system that we had formerly used was to let each department carry, whenever it was physically possible, a complete stock of the stationery it used. The overflow was put in bins. Apparently in order to simplify the task of finding supplies, a sample form was pasted on the outside of each bin.

All that the stock boy had to do was to walk up one aisle and down the other, carefully searching for the sample! Of course, the stock boy knew where the most important items were kept, but it was not always possible for a person in search of stationery to find where the stock boy kept himself. Again, if the stock boy did not forget, he usually told the purchasing agent when the stock was running low on any particular item. If he did forget, he got "a terrible scolding" and perhaps a whole department was held up until the printer could send a new supply.

To remedy this condition, we first set aside a certain portion of the office as a storeroom. No department now is allowed to keep on hand more than a couple of days' supply of any form. All the rest is sent to the storeroom. Then an inventory was taken and symbols were given to all forms.

We use a "balance of stores" loose-leaf record. This serves as a perpetual in-

THIS TABLE SAVES 25% OF A GIRL'S TIME

A special study which Mr. Leffingwell made of mail-opening resulted in designing this table, which enables the clerk to do her work in a fourth less time than formerly. Note especially the convenient foot-rest, and the sunken paper tray and pin cushions

ventory. A "low limit" is set for each form or article and instructions are written on each sheet that when the stock falls to this limit a requisition for a certain fixed quantity must be issued.

This record has the usual columns for "stores apportioned" and "stores issued," and I shall describe how we use those columns. Whenever, for example, we decide to issue a certain form letter in a certain quantity, for which letterheads will be needed, the number necessary is entered in the "stores apportioned" column. This of course reduces the "available" supplies just that much. If it brings our normal supply below the "low limit" we order more at once. Thus we never have the humiliating experience of using up all "available" supplies by some sudden and unforeseen decision.

Our next step was to arrange the stock so that it could be found with a minimum of labor, not only by the regular stock boy, but by a substitute. We had it placed in numbered bins, or on shelves, according to the kind of supply. Then we made a very completely cross-indexed card record of locations. This record is indexed as follows:

1. By symbol
2. By name
3. By department
4. By approximate name or class name (for example, all envelopes are together)

In addition, the "balance of stores" record shows, immediately under the symbol, which bin contains the desired form.

When the purchasing department orders stores a copy of the purchasing order goes to the planning department, to be entered on the "balance of stores" record. When stores are received notice is sent both to the purchasing department and the planning department.

We placed the storeroom in charge of one person, and no stores are issued without an order from the planning department. The planning department keeps the "balance of stores" record and, in addition, charges all stationery used by a department to a special stationery account. This latter record is for cost purposes. It enables the management to know more about that bugbear "overhead."

After the organization had been thoroughly standardized and operation times were known, we next took up the work of routing and scheduling.

One of the important considerations in getting work through the various operations is to avoid "necks," or places where the work is likely to become congested. Congestion can be avoided only by knowing just how long it takes to perform each operation. If one operation for any reason requires much more time than others, special attention should be paid to it. Otherwise the work will pile up.

Perhaps the best way to explain our entire system of routing will be to describe in detail how we route our orders.

We found that much time could be saved by sorting the orders into classes. Special clerks, therefore, were placed in the planning department to do this sorting and classifying. They put the orders in envelopes in bunches of twenty-four of one kind. On the outside of the envelope is clipped what we call a route sheet (see below).

This route sheet contains a number. Each order inside is stamped with a numbering machine, with the twenty-four individual numbers following the last "hundreds" figure in the route sheet number. For example, if the route sheet number is 15,400 the orders inside the

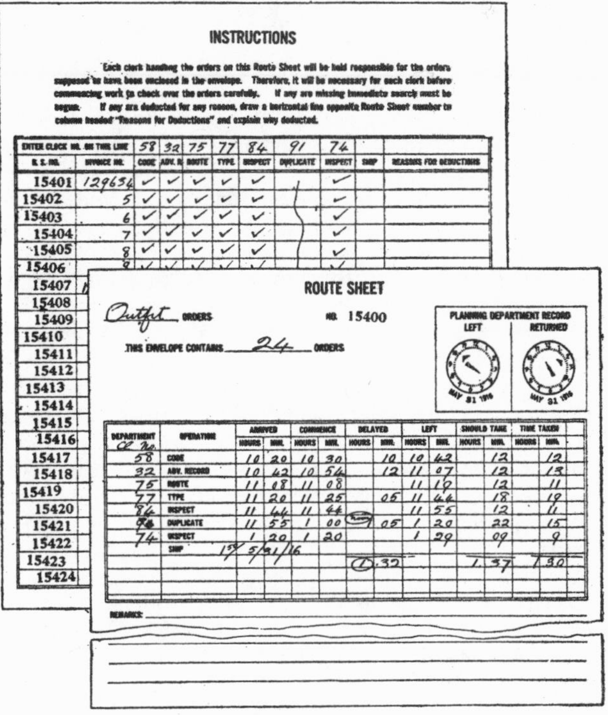

INSTRUCTIONS

Each clerk handling the orders on this Route Sheet will be held responsible for the orders supposed to have been enclosed in the envelope. Therefore, it will be necessary for each clerk before commencing work to check over the orders carefully. If any are missing immediate search must be begun. If any are deducted for any reason, draw a horizontal line opposite Route Sheet number to column headed "Reasons for Deductions" and explain why deducted.

ENTER CLOCK NO. ON THIS LINE		58	32	75	77	84	91	74		
R. S. NO.	INVOICE NO.	CODE	ADV. R.	ROUTE	TYPE	INSPECT	DUPLICATE	INSPECT	SHIP	REASONS FOR DEDUCTIONS
15401	129634	✓	✓	✓	✓	✓		✓		
15402	5	✓	✓	✓	✓	✓		✓		
15403	6	✓	✓	✓	✓	✓		✓		
15404	7	✓	✓	✓	✓	✓		✓		
15405	8	✓	✓	✓	✓	✓		✓		
15406	9	✓	✓	✓	✓	✓		✓		
15407										
15408										
15409										
15410										
15411										
15412										
15413										
15414										
15415										
15416										
15417										
15418										
15419										
15420										
15421										
15422										
15423										
15424										

ROUTE SHEET

Outfit ORDERS NO. 15400

THIS ENVELOPE CONTAINS 24 ORDERS

PLANNING DEPARTMENT RECORD
LEFT: MAY 31 1916
RETURNED: MAY 31 1916

DEPARTMENT Cl. No.	OPERATION	ARRIVED HOURS	ARRIVED MIN.	COMMENCE HOURS	COMMENCE MIN.	DELAYED HOURS	DELAYED MIN.	LEFT HOURS	LEFT MIN.	SHOULD TAKE HOURS	SHOULD TAKE MIN.	TIME TAKEN HOURS	TIME TAKEN MIN.
58	CODE	10	20	10	30		10	10	42		12		12
32	ADV. RECORD	10	42	10	54		12	11	07		12		13
75	ROUTE	11	08	11	08			11	19		12		11
77	TYPE	11	20	11	25		05	11	44		18		19
84	INSPECT	11	44	11	44			11	55		12		11
[illegible]	DUPLICATE	11	55	1	00	[illegible]	05	1	20		22		15
74	INSPECT	1	20	1	20			1	29		09		9
	SHIP	1 5/31/16											
						(1).32				1.37		1.30	

REMARKS:

THESE SHEETS "KEEP TIME" ON WORK

A sheet like this (the front and reverse are shown above) are pinned to each batch of orders. They help the planning clerk keep the work moving properly through the departments

envelope will be numbered from 15,401 to 15,424. Thus the last two figures always indicate the number of the order and the other figures the route sheet number.

Before the orders leave the mail opening department they have been given a number (stamped in red ink) and are at once listed by a typist in exact numerical order on a numerical register. When the planning department clerks route the orders they write the number of the route sheet opposite the original number in the numerical register. In this way we are sure that every order received is routed.

When the order is routed it is thereafter counted as one portion of a unit of work – the unit being twenty-four orders. For each operation thereafter there is a definite task. That is to say, we know how much time should be taken. Immediately a route sheet is sent on its way, the order-of-work clerk in the planning department places a black-headed pin on the planning board for each clerk who will handle that route sheet. She places the pins ahead for the exact number of minutes required.. Thus each operation is planned and definite work scheduled for each employee. If the planning board shows that one clerk already has more than one hour's work ahead, some other clerk is chosen.

As soon as a route sheet arrives in a department the time is stamped on a small slip of paper containing the number of the route sheet and the name of the department. When it leaves the department the time is again stamped and the slip at once put in the messenger box and returned on the next trip to the planning department. When this slip arrives in the planning department the order of work clerk notes the information on a special record. Thus, within fifteen minutes of that time the planning department knows just what department has the route sheet. If there is any delay at any point it is at once detected and an investigation made. The large bulk of our orders are packed and ready for shipment in less than two hours after they leave the mail opening department.

After the route sheet returns from the shipping department another record is taken of the times actually required on all operations as shown on the face of the route sheet. Each day we thereby know the actual labor spent on the orders, and can estimate to the smallest fraction the comparative effectiveness of our record.

Of course, it must be understood that this system is particularly applicable to our own business. In some other lines it would have to be planned to cover specific conditions. In my opinion, however, in its essentials such a system can be applied to almost any office work.

HOW OFFICE EMPLOYEES LIKE "SCIENTIFIC MANAGEMENT"

Once an employee is put on our permanent payroll we are very reluctant indeed about discharging him. If there is sufficient work for him we take every effort to make him a valuable employee. The teachers and time study men are in most cases able to fit employees for the work and, on standardized operations, get them to earning a bonus within a month or so. We prefer, wherever it is possible, to advance employees who are working on unstandardized operations to the vacancies which will make it possible for them to earn bonus money. Such an advancement is considered a promotion. In most cases new employees are given unstandardized positions.

In some positions which require a great deal of training, we make a practice of having several understudies, any one of whom is ready to take hold of the work at once in case of an emergency.

The question of increases in salary, which in most establishments is a vexing one, we do not find difficult because those who are earning bonus money are earning more than they could get in similar positions with other houses and have no desire to leave us. They know that they are paid well for good work; and we are glad to pay them well, for it benefits us in many ways to do so.

41 WAYS
TO SAVE TIME IN AN OFFICE

William H. Leffingwell

TIRED EYES CANNOT DO THE BEST WORK

Artificial light, unless it is properly handled, may cause much eye strain. The light should not be placed below the level of the eyes, as it is in the picture shown above, but should come from high above the head and in sufficient quantity to cause even illumination

41 WAYS TO SAVE TIME IN AN OFFICE

Very often, as this article points out, it's the "little wastes," the ones so trifling that you are inclined to think they hardly count, that roll up the biggest total of lost effort in the end

By WM. H. LEFFINGWELL

Illustrated with PHOTOGRAPHS

MISDIRECTED motions mean waste wherever they appear. In many offices, for some reason or other, less attention is usually directed to waste motions than in other branches of business activity.

Still, work goes to waste in offices as well as in manufacturing or sales rooms.

The layout of the office itself, for instance, may not encourage effective work. It is impossible, of course, to lay out a definite blanket plan to be followed in the physical arrangement of all offices. But it is safe to lay out almost any office in about the same way that an expert plans a factory.

You can, for instance, make a diagram of your office as it is today, showing each desk in its present position. Then you can draw lines showing the passage of the work from desk to desk. You may be surprised, unless your office is unusually well organized, to see how many times those lines cross and turn back upon themselves. Nothing will show you so clearly the wasted steps which your employees may be taking.

If letters weighed ten pounds apiece, probably a correct routing would quickly enough be found. But because they usually weigh but an ounce or so, failures to attain a direct routing are often not observed. It takes nearly as much time, however, to carry one ounce one hundred feet as to carry ten pounds. The illustration on page 141 shows how a great deal of waste motion was eliminated in one office where this plan of study and rearrangement was tried.

In planning an office, the relation of one department to another should be closely studied. The work wants to flow in a continuous direction wherever possible.

Consideration should also be given to future growth. Do not lay out an office on an ideal plan that is likely to be upset by the growth of the business.

Poor arrangement is not the only cause of wasted motions in offices, however. In fact, there are many causes, some of which are often not given much attention simply because they are so commonplace that they are thought unworthy of attention. Some of the more serious of these causes will be pointed out in this article, together with the remedies that usually bring results.

For instance, there are interruptions. Office work can not be done effectively if there are many interruptions.

Noises are prevalent disturbers – not only the unusual noises, but also the

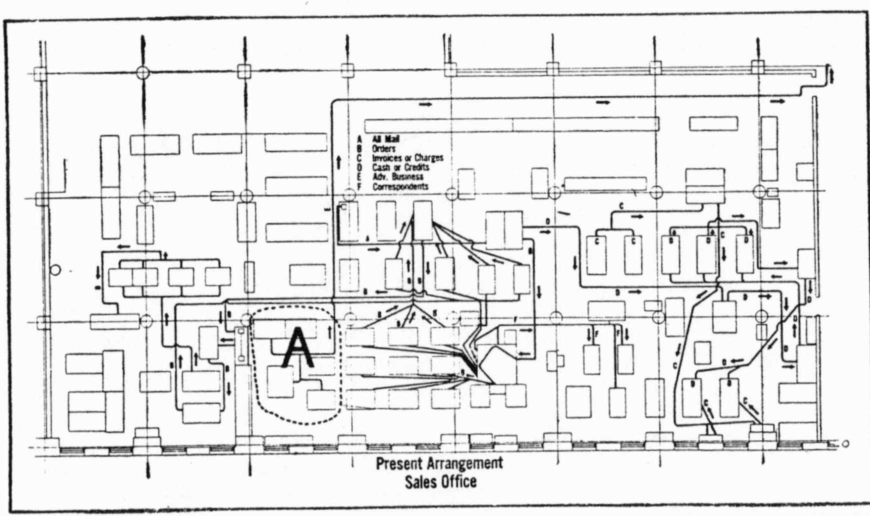

A POOR OFFICE LAYOUT–

Many offices, like Topsy, have "just growed." Above is shown a study made in one such office. The heavy lines show the direction in which work travels from desk to desk, and it is easy to see how it takes long jumps and loops back on itself. The five desks shown at "A" had practically nothing to do with the work at the other desks in the room, and one girl who was placed there had to travel to an entirely different part of the office, not shown above, about twenty times a day

noises that occur constantly. In an office located in a large factory the clerks worked on the first floor. In the basement was the punch press department, while the machine shop was on the second floor. Added to the regular noise of the factory was the noise of a dozen or more typewriters and a few other office devices. The noise was constant and, after a few days, employees apparently became hardened to it. When I mentioned this, the manager stated that the girls were used to it and "never noticed it."

I made an experiment. Two of the typists were assigned to a room where there was much less noise. One girl increased her output ninety per cent, and another one hundred per cent! The experiment convinced the manager that the noise was really expensive.

In another office I have seen fifty clerks lose a quarter of a minute every time a truck rolled across the floor above them. That particular truck made two or three trips an hour. Figured out, that meant a loss of sixty thousand minutes in a year, or one thousand hours. At even twenty cents an hour, this loss amounted to two hundred dollars and would have bought many pairs of rubber tires for the offending truck.

Then there are interruptions caused by distraction. Dozens of times I have seen offices so arranged that visitors were interviewed within plain sight and hearing of the whole office. When there is loud talking, usually everyone must listen, whether he wishes to or not. And the listening causes a waste of time, poor work, and mistakes.

Every interruption of whatever kind not only causes a delay during the actual interruption, but on account of the effort required to get back into the swing of the work, considerable extra time. Important delays can also often be avoided by messenger systems, well-placed drinking fountains, arrangements for supplying work and stationery, and office regulations which keep the clerks at work instead of

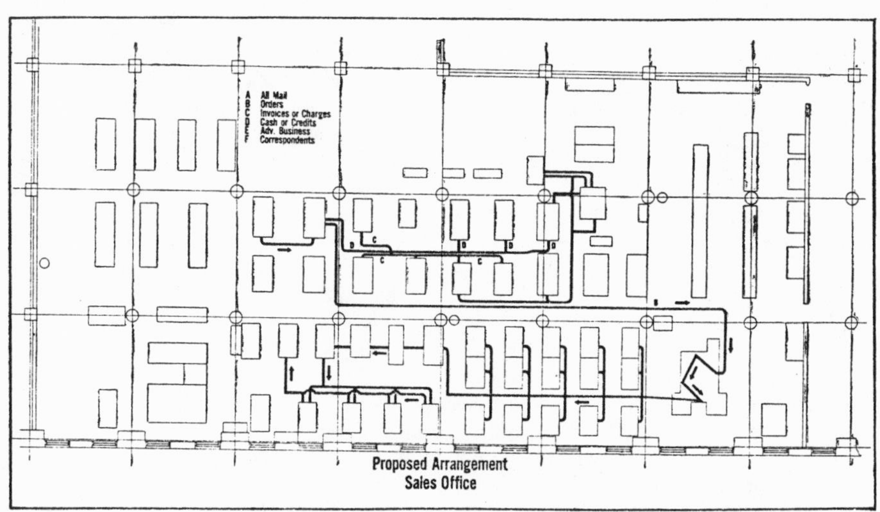

-AND THE SAME OFFICE, REARRANGED

This is the same office as the one shown on the opposite page, rearranged to allow the work to move in straight lines. A glance at this layout, in comparison with the original arrangement, shows how the work has been simplified. Desks are so placed as to leave convenient aisles, and permit the handling of papers without having them carried backwards and forwards unnecessarily. The desks at "A" in the other layout have been transferred to another part of the office, and three drinking fountains installed in place of two

running about or talking too much to one another.

Another common cause of wasted motion is the lack of effective equipment. By this I do not necessarily mean only office machines, but even such common needs as rulers, pens, inkwells, scratch-pads, pencils and the like. These supplies are cheap, yet office managers will sometimes try to economize on them and compel clerks to waste time, which is often of more value than the supplies in question, borrowing from one another what each should have. I have seen clerks waste from five to ten minutes a day in this way. Usually it did not take this long to do the actual borrowing, but the need furnished an opportunity to talk or to ask useless questions. A loss of five minutes a day by a ten-dollar-a-week clerk amounts to over five dollars a year: a sum that would buy quite a stock of supplies.

DO YOUR CLERKS HAVE THE EQUIPMENT BEST SUITED TO THEIR WORK?

Insufficient filing space is a cause of waste motion in many offices. It is not unusual to see files crowded so full of papers and letters that the actual labor necessary for filing is doubled or even trebled. I have seen instances where doubling the number of filing cabinets has cut in half the number of filing clerks.

In filing cards, too little thought is sometimes devoted to the number of guide cards necessary. It is true that guide cards take up space, and they are comparatively expensive. But neither the equipment nor the space is so expensive as the time that may be wasted hunting for cards. If a filing clerk could put her finger upon the right card the first time, it would not take long to locate cards. But, as a matter of fact, the average filing clerk makes several attempts before she locates the right card. Every attempt that fails to locate the right card is wasted, and several of them can be avoided. Sufficient guide cards of the right sort will often increase the output from fifty to two hundred per cent.

It seems ridiculous to say that some offices provide an insufficient number of chairs. Yet a clerk may often waste considerable time looking for his particular chair. Someone has borrowed it to use at an idle desk for a moment, or for a caller. It pays every office to have a chair for every table or desk, whether occupied or not, and to keep that chair there all the time.

Here is another detail – minutes are often wasted borrowing a knife to sharpen a pencil. It pays to have a good pencil-sharpening machine at each desk. This, however, may be unnecessary, for the office boy, in a few minutes, with a good machine, can sharpen a great many pencils. Each clerk should always have several sharpened pencils on his desk.

Again, there are telephones. The initial expense of installing a comprehensive telephone system sometimes hinders managers from putting in the equipment. But this initial expense may be paid out many times in the wages representing time lost by clerks.

In installing telephones, I have found it wise not to limit them to department managers. Some clerks are consulted oftener than the managers. This is frequently the case when the clerk uses the department manager's telephone – the manager has to answer it and then call the clerk! The clerk comes to the manager's desk, and while talking disturbs him. This wastes the time of both.

I have mentioned only a few of the motions wasted by insufficient equipment. The list could easily be lengthened. Another type of loss may occur when the equipment provided is poor, or poorly kept up.

Take chairs, for instance. Any kind of a chair is often considered satisfactory, as long as it holds together. Usually, too little attention is paid to the fact that people are of different sizes and shapes. Some have long legs and short bodies; some have short legs and long bodies;

others have long legs and long bodies, or short legs and short bodies.

All are usually supposed to use chairs of the same size. Short persons can often do better work and more of it if their chairs are raised an inch or so by a leather cushion. Foot stools will often reduce fatigue. About as much is true of desks. Many managers are evidently unaware that manufacturers of office equipment are turning out some very modern desks nowadays.

Makeshift transfer cabinets, bad letter files, bad card files and the like, may waste sufficient time to pay for the very best sort of equipment. Every piece of equipment that is not at least seventy-five per cent effective should, I am convinced, be junked without compunction.

Bad lighting is another condition that may receive too little consideration. In many offices, all available windows are used for the private offices, the occupants of which may do but little reading, while the dark spaces beyond are assigned to clerks who must read and write all day by artificial light.

Artificial light, being as a rule highly concentrated, may cause much eye strain unless properly handled. In one concern order blanks were made of a calendered paper which reflected the strong electric light back into the eyes of the clerks. The orders here were written in pencil, and much time was lost by shifting the paper around to avoid the glare.

If artificial light must be used, it is important that it come from high above the head and in sufficient quantity to cause even illumination. There should be no dark corners nor heavy shadows. It is a mistake to place the light close to the work and below the eye level of the clerk, for even though it is shaded, the pupils of the eye must adjust themselves to the darkness when looking up. This often results in considerable strain.

Clerks with bad eyesight or strained and tired eyes can not do their best work, and no office can afford to have anything but the very best light and lighting equipment. If electric lights are used, it is important to have the lamps frequently cleaned and periodically inspected, for a lamp will often burn long after it has lost the larger part of its effectiveness.

MAKING THE TOP LINES EASY TO READ

Sometimes the remedy for waste motion may be very simple. In one case, placing a little box under a huge ledger, as shown above, saved a bookkeeper hundreds of needless movements daily

Wherever possible, good daylight should be furnished to clerks who must use their eyes eight or more hours a day for reading and writing. Plenty of white paint can also be advantageously used on the walls, and the windows should be kept thoroughly cleaned.

You may insist that these suggestions are trite. Nevertheless, in my experience, few offices seem really to appreciate the value of good light sufficiently to get it. Poor lighting facilities have, however, an effect upon the efficiency of workers that can be computed in dollars and cents. Very few offices, furthermore, have satisfactory ventilation systems – read the article on page 323 of SYSTEM for September of last year if you want technical proof of the value of an effective ventilation system.

When there are several motions in any one operation, these motions should always be performed in the same order in order to get the highest output. If this is not done there is a waste. Constant repetition of the same sequence of motions establishes rhythm, usually increases speed and lessens errors.

In one case a clerk had to use a rubber stamp, then a pencil, then a numbering machine, and finally she had to pin and place the work aside. Observation showed that sometimes she used the pencil first, and sometimes the rubber stamp. At other times she would do the pinning before she used the rubber stamp.

HOW THE ELIMINATION OF EXTRA MOTIONS ENABLED A GIRL TO DO 25% MORE WORK

This lack of sequence led to her placing the rubber stamp and the numbering machine in different places each time. The loss of time from this cause could only be measured by hundredths of a minute, but it amounted to considerable in a day because the operation was constantly being repeated.

She was then taught to perform the work in the same sequence all the time, with the result that her efficiency was increased twenty-five per cent. It pays to make a very careful investigation into the best methods and, when the one best way has been discovered, to teach it to all who perform that particular task.

As a rule, office work consists of several different operations, usually performed by different persons. For example, when the mail is received it follows some such course as this:

1. Mail opened
2. Cash balanced
3. Orders read and interpreted
4. Invoiced
5. Recorded
6. Filled
7. Packed and shipped

Of course these steps are not identical in all offices, but the routine is usually similar.

Now, the method of routing has an important bearing on results. If some of these operations require more work than others, care must be used. Just as the careful factory manager does not give a machine more work than it is capable of handling, so the office manager should not give clerks more than they can do. The speed with which an order travels through the house is fixed by the speed of the longest operation.

If care is used, it is nearly always possible to divide the operations so that each requires about the same amount of time. The short ones can be combined to make one operation, and the long ones divided or additional help directed toward them.

Suppose one piece of work requires seven operations that are performed in the following times:

1st operation	1 minute
2nd operation	½ minute
3rd operation	½ minute
4th operation	2 minutes
5th operation	1 minute
6th operation	1 minute
7th operation	2½ minutes
Total time	8½ minutes

It is evident that the theoretical time necessary is eight and one-half minutes; but it is easily possible, with faulty routing, for this work to require fourteen and one-half minutes, six minutes of which is wasted and can be avoided.

But if operations two and three are combined, and operation four is divided into two operations, and two persons are put on operation seven, there will be no waste whatsoever. The actual time will equal the theoretical time. This is simply a matter of arithmetic. It is often the case in offices, however, that operators will slow down unconsciously while waiting for slow operations to be finished, and it will actually seem logical that the entire work requires fourteen minutes.

The work should travel regularly and smoothly with no waits between operations. That is the ideal condition. If, on analysis, it appears that one operation requires much more time than another, that particular operation should be studied carefully to see if it can be shortened or divided. If not, I always make it a point to put extra people on that particular work so as to keep the line moving regularly.

THIS CLERK'S OUTPUT WAS TRIPLED

In even so simple an operation as opening mail there is a right and a wrong way. Mr. Leffingwell tells, on page 147, how the output of one clerk engaged on this task was increased from 80 letters to 250 letters an hour

The number of pieces of work put through at a time can also be studied carefully and arranged to suit the needs of the business. It is evident that even with ideal routing a piece of work consisting of ten operations, requiring one minute each, can not be rushed through in ten minutes without a messenger being available to pass it along from one worker to the other. On the other hand, if sixty pieces are given to each worker, and they are not passed along until finished, it would require ten hours for the lot to pass through all hands. So, each business must decide just how many pieces shall be routed at a time.

Houses which make a specialty of shipping promptly often pass the orders along in small lots, which are so arranged that every order arriving before a certain hour will leave the house the same day it is received. These orders have a definite time schedule, and if the schedule is rigidly followed it is a great help to rapid output.

Another source of waste motions is lack of standardization of printed matter used in the office. Every office uses certain forms. These grow in number, usually, as the office grows in years. Sometimes, because of changing conditions, forms may become antiquated without being discarded. It is well, therefore, to have all of the forms brought together and standardized by someone who knows the entire routine of the office.

Usually such an investigation shows that a number of the forms can be discontinued altogether, some may be combined with others, and all can be standardized in size, shape, and make-up. After a thorough clean-up of this kind it is surprising how much labor can often be saved, to say nothing of the saving through reduced printing bills. It is impossible, of course, to give specific rules for this work, since no two offices are exactly alike, but the following ideas may be suggestive:

First, in gathering the forms for inspection, endeavor to get forms that have been filled out in the regular way. Look for unfilled spaces. These will usually indicate whether or not that particular information is at present used or desired.

Second, gather the forms by departments – often it will be found that two or three forms can be combined into one.

Third, if any forms are obsolete, find out as nearly as possible their original use. I have often found that a very good system was started and then for some unaccountable reason discontinued. Find out why the discarded systems are obsolete.

Fourth, trace the object of every form and see if it is thoroughly accomplishing that object. Perhaps you will find that the clerk is writing, hundreds of times a day, information which should have been printed on the blank.

Fifth, if the forms are reports which are later filed in a book, endeavor as far as possible to standardize in size so as to have uniform binders. Better prices can generally be secured if binders are bought in quantities. Besides, there is much wasted motion in storing and getting at binders of all shapes and sizes.

Sixth, interview the users of all forms and see if they have any suggestions about improvements. Do not adopt any suggestions, however, without finding what effect these changes will have on the rest of the work.

Seventh, study carefully each blank, with the idea of limiting the amount of writing as much as possible. Get all of the writing bunched together. Get numbers in the corner where they can easily be read, if possible.

Standardization means reducing the number of forms, increasing the effectiveness of those used, cutting the printing bill, the storage space and the time required for locating and storing. It often also means the discovery of a waste of hundreds of dollars in wages spent for making out forms which are obsolete.

Often printed forms require certain information to be written in by the clerk. As much of this can be standardized, usually a number of standard sentences can be printed on the form and a check mark, placed opposite the information it is desired to convey, will do the work quite as well, and very much more quickly, than writing. Where it is not possible to use this plan, much time can often be saved by having a number of rubber stamps that will take the place of writing by hand.

The pinning or clipping of papers is another problem that comes up in nearly every office. Few clerks, it seems, know how to pin papers so that everything but the top sheet can be read without unpinning. Often the sheets are pinned two or three inches from the top. The next person who must read the papers has to un-pin and re-pin them.

It is simple, with a bit of study, to see that the pinning is done right in the first place. Different classes of papers, of course, may have to be pinned differently. Some require the envelope on top, some on the bottom, some demand a particular sequence, and so on. The problem is worth careful study, for the thousands of papers handled in the average office have to be pinned on an average of five or six times, if there is no general rule of pinning right in the first place. This means a loss of possibly from .05 to .10 of a minute for each pinning. If 1,000 sets of papers are handled in a day, and pinned and re-pinned half a dozen times, this amounts to from three hundred to six hundred minutes a day – a total loss.

In many cases a simple pasting operation will save much time and many pins. In one instance, pasting saved twenty-five per cent of the time of several clerks.

SOME SIMPLE WAYS TO PREVENT THE LOSS OF ENERGY

Typists should always have some kind of a copy holder adaptable for the needs of their work. The number of times the neck has to be twisted by the average typist working without a copy holder is appalling.

In the same way, clerks working on huge books often exert enough physical energy peering into the binder margin to make a pig iron loader tired. They twist about, working not only the muscles of the neck but of the back, perhaps thousands of times a day.

Much of this energy can be avoided by using simple equipment. In one instance we found that by simply placing a small box under one end of a heavy book which opened end-wise, we raised up the back end and made it possible to see the top-most lines. This simple arrangement saved the clerk from leaning over eighteen inches and back again on an average of one hundred times an hour. In one working day that clerk formerly moved his back a distance of nearly half a mile.

I have also frequently watched inspectors who were comparing addresses. They will often have the work in two separate piles at least a foot apart. This necessitates a twist of the head many thousands of times a day. By moving the two piles of work closer together, the same work can be accomplished by simply shifting the eyes, which is less fatiguing.

As a rule, the employer leaves the employee to chose his own method of doing his work. The results are often bad. I have, for instance, seen girls enclosing letters at the rate of fifteen hundred an hour, working alongside of girls who were enclosing two hundred an hour. It pays in any office to spend plenty of time teaching employees the most effective way of doing things.

Expert card filers have a simple little trick of taking out a few cards from the place where the card they are searching ought to be. Then with a simple rapid downward movement of the thumb, which is hard to describe, they locate the desired card in less time than it takes to tell about it. Inexperienced filers will run their fingers over the tops of the cards, looking at first one and then another, separating the cards with a finger nail. This method accomplishes less than one-fifth the work accomplished by the former. Yet, in nearly any office where the problem has not received attention, not only will you find these two methods, as a rule, but several others even less skillful.

When papers or letters are to be filed away, they should be properly sorted in the beginning, either alphabetically or numerically. This saves much more time than it takes to sort them. The same principle can be adapted to many kinds of work. If it is necessary to look up certain items in a card file, for instance, it nearly always pays to sort the work first. Yet it is seldom that you find clerks carrying this idea out completely, for they usually wish to begin the "real work" as soon as possible.

HOW THE WORK OF OPENING MAIL WAS SIMPLIFIED

Again, many operations can be divided so that one motion is performed a number of times in succession. This will usually increase the speed, and should be done wherever possible.

In one case – opening mail – the work which followed the cutting of the envelopes with a machine was as follows:

1. Letters taken out of envelope
2. Envelope pinned to papers
3. Money, if any, detached and put away
4. Rubber stamped, and amount of money marked with a pencil
5. If no money was enclosed, this stamp was used: "No money enclosed"

This method was thorough enough, but it was necessary with each letter to pick up the rubber stamp, lay it down, pick up the pencil, mark and lay it down. The output was eighty letters an hour.

By omitting – at the time of opening – the rubber stamping of the letters which contained no money, and by laying them all in a basket and stamping them at the end of each mail sorted, the output was increased to two hundred and fifty per hour. This new method was taught to all employees and in a few days all were working at the higher rate of speed, with the result that the mail was ready for attention soon after it arrived.

Instances of waste motion could no doubt be multiplied almost indefinitely. Some of those that have been mentioned are so obvious that it would seem they could scarcely escape attention. Yet the fact that they do is evidenced in dozens of offices, where oftentimes even more obvious sources of loss pass without being remedied. It pays to keep a close watch for many of these losses.

HISTORY OF MANAGEMENT THOUGHT

An Arno Press Collection

Arnold, Horace Lucian. **The Complete Cost-Keeper.** 1901

Austin, Bertram and W. Francis Lloyd. **The Secret of High Wages.** 1926

Berriman, A. E., et al. **Industrial Administration.** 1920

Cadbury, Edward. **Experiments In Industrial Organization.** 1912

Carlson, Sune. **Executive Behaviour.** 1951

Carney, Edward M. et al. **The American Business Manual.** 1914

Casson, Herbert N. **Factory Efficiency.** 1917

Chandler, Alfred D., editor. **The Application of Modern Systematic Management.** 1979

Chandler, Alfred D., editor. **Management Thought in Great Britain.** 1979

Chandler, Alfred D., editor. **Managerial Innovation at General Motors.** 1979

Chandler, Alfred D., editor. **Pioneers in Modern Factory Management.** 1979

Chandler, Alfred D., editor. **Precursors of Modern Management.** 1979

Chandler, Alfred D., editor. **The Railroads.** 1979

Church, A. Hamilton. **The Proper Distribution Of Expense Burden.** 1908

Davis, Ralph Currier. **The Fundamentals Of Top Management.** 1951

Devinat, Paul. **Scientific Management In Europe.** 1927

Diemer, Hugo. **Factory Organization and Administration.** 1910 and 1935

Elbourne, Edward T. **Factory Administration and Accounts.** 1919

Elbourne, Edward T. **Fundamentals of Industrial Administration.** 1934

Emerson, Harrington. **Efficiency as a Basis for Operation and Wages.** 1909

Kirkman, Marshall M[onroe]. **Railway Revenue.** 1879

Kirkman, Marshall M[onroe]. **Railway Expenditures.** 1880

Laurence, Edward. **The Duty and Office of a Land Steward.** 1731

Lee, John. **Management.** 1921

Lee, John, editor. **Pitman's Dictionary of Industrial Administration.** 1928

McKinsey, James O. **Managerial Accounting.** 1924

Rowntree, B. Seebohm. **The Human Factor in Business.** 1921

Schell, Erwin Haskell. **The Technique of Executive Control.** 1924

Sheldon, Oliver. **The Philosophy of Management.** 1923

Tead, Ordway and Henry C. Metcalfe. **Personnel Administration.** 1926

Urwick, L[yndall]. **The Golden Book of Management.** 1956

Urwick, L[yndall]. **Management of Tomorrow.** 1933